INTERLIBRARY LOAN PROCEDURE MANUAL

SARAH KATHARINE THOMSON

Interlibrary Loan Committee
Reference Services Division
American Library Association
Chicago 1970

International Standard Book Number 0-8389-3113-8 (1970)
Library of Congress Catalog Card Number 71-125942
Copyright © 1970 by the American Library Association
Printed in the United States of America

INTERLIBRARY LOAN COMMITTEE
Reference Services Division

American Library Association

Contents

Figures

Appendixes

Preface

This manual has as its purposes the interpretation of policy stated in the "National Interlibrary Loan Code, 1968"; the presentation of standardized, efficient methods of transacting interlibrary loan; and the explanation of details of procedure to be followed.

The "National Interlibrary Loan Code, 1968" is designed to make nationally held bibliographic resources as widely available as possible and, at the same time, to protect the interests of the primary readers in the lending libraries. Following the policies of the code and the procedures specified in this manual will result in a higher proportion of filled requests and will speed and ease the processing of requests especially in large libraries.

Attitudes and practices regarding interlibrary loan differ among the various types of libraries: academic libraries, state and public libraries, and special libraries, particularly medical libraries. Nevertheless, the elements of good interlibrary loan work—verification, citation, and location—are the same regardless of the types of libraries or the media used. Usually libraries borrow most heavily from other libraries of their own type; yet the major academic libraries, because of the strength of their collections, act as back-up resources to all.

Networks are employing a variety of devices to speed materials: teletypewriter communication; switching, referral, and relay arrangements; printed catalogs and union lists; delivery services; direct loans to readers on a reciprocal basis; and automatic photocopy substitution.

The American Library Association in its "Goals for Action" proposed the establishment of networks between libraries to make available to all citizens the full range of research resources. Since demand for library materials is far in excess of supply in both personnel and resources, and since interlibrary lending is costly, some regulation of demand is necessary. Each borrowing and each lending library has an obligation to screen requests toward optimal allocation of these limited resources. Some librarians regard the access to information as a right and consider the furtherance of knowledge on all levels to be in the public interest. Others think that borrowing libraries should recognize that they are asking a favor, that interlibrary loan is a courtesy and a privilege, and that adherence to codified principles and practices is in the common interest.

Any organized library staffed by an authorized person can participate in interlibrary loan. Librarians are urged to request the editor of the *American*

Library Directory to list their library to facilitate interlibrary loan transactions.

Every library has the right to specify conditions of loan and to decline to lend specific materials. Each lending library has an obligation to establish priorities of user demands upon its collections. In general, these priorities are:

1) Public library: a) its community, b) other libraries in its system, users from other libraries in its system, c) other libraries in the same state, d) out of state libraries.

2) College library: a) its faculty, students, research, staff, b) local community, other libraries in its system, c) other academic libraries, d) libraries in general.

3) University library: a) its faculty, students, research, staff, b) other libraries in its system, academic and research personnel in its area, c) other academic libraries, d) other libraries.

4) Special library: a) personnel of its organization, b) affiliated organizations, c) other special libraries and· university libraries from which it borrows, d) other libraries.[1]

Information on interlibrary lending of serials and dissertations has been included in the *Directory of Institutional Photocopying Services (Including Selected Interlibrary Loan Policies),* compiled by Cosby Brinkley (Chicago, 1969).

The INTERLIBRARY LOAN PROCEDURE MANUAL will be used by librarians of varying levels of sophistication: library school students and novice interlibrary loan librarians as well as highly skilled and experienced professionals. It may also be used by technical assistants and clerical personnel assigned to interlibrary loan work. Therefore it has been arranged for quick consultation and with emphasis on some basic procedures that veteran librarians may consider elementary and obvious; similarly, repetition in the section on use of the Interlibrary Loan Request form, especially citation requirements, is deliberate.

This manual has been prepared with the assistance, advice, and approval of the ALA Reference Services Division Interlibrary Loan Committee. Committee members who participated in the conference on the National Interlibrary Loan Code held in Chicago on December 2–3, 1967, were: Marjorie Karlson, chairman, who wrote the initial draft, Miriam Allen, James C. Andrews, John Andrew Fisher, Phoebe F. Hayes, David W. Heron, Charles G. LaHood, Arthur McAnally, Michael M. Reynolds, George A. Schwegmann, Jr., Jane Titus, Lucien White, and Sarah Katharine Thomson, consultant. William R. Gordon and Legare H. B. Obear became members of the committee in 1969. Many people offered valuable advice and assistance, especially Ellis Mount and Hubert E. Sauter on technical reports; Eugene P. Sheehy on international borrowing and

---

[1]Quoted from Margaret D. Uridge's table "Priority of Library Users" distributed to members of the Institute for Training in Librarianship for Interlibrary Loan Librarians, Oct. 13, 1969, University of Colorado, Boulder.

lending; Miwa Kai on non-Roman-alphabet requests; Patricia Colling on doctoral dissertations from University Microfilms; Warren Bird on teletypewriter transactions; Mary Ellis Kahler and George A. Schwegmann, Jr., on requests to the Union Catalog Division of the Library of Congress; Joseph H. Treyz and the members of the executive committee of the Reproduction of Library Materials Section of RTSD on copying, copyright, and lending to reprinters; and Phoebe F. Hayes and the directors of the union catalogs and bibliographical centers who responded to the questionnaires. Marjorie Karlson compiled the abbreviations list of verification sources, and Phoebe F. Hayes had primary responsibility for drafting the model local code and for the annotations to it in chapter 2. James C. Andrews, Patricia Ballou, Phoebe F. Hayes, Marjorie Karlson, Georgia Pribanic, Elizabeth Rumics, and Jane Titus read the manuscript thoroughly at various stages and made valuable comments.

With the permission of the Reference Services Division Board of Directors, six chapters from this manual were distributed to the participants at the Institute for Training in Librarianship for Interlibrary Loan Librarians at the University of Colorado at Boulder on October 13–17, 1969. Many helpful suggestions from the presentations of the faculty have been incorporated into this manual, especially from Warren Bird, Virginia Boucher, Maryann Duggan, Phoebe F. Hayes, Russell Shank, and Margaret D. Uridge.

SARAH KATHARINE THOMSON

1/National Interlibrary Loan Code, 1968, Annotated

INTRODUCTION

This code, adopted by the Reference Services Division, acting for the American Library Association on June 27, 1968, governs the interlibrary lending relations among libraries on the national level, among research libraries, and among libraries not operating under special or local codes. Libraries of a common geographical area or those specializing in the same field may find it advantageous to develop codes for their own needs. There is appended to this national code a model state code[1] which may be considered for adoption by such groups of libraries with common interests.

On the national level interlibrary loan requests should be restricted to materials which cannot be obtained readily and at moderate cost by other means. The costs involved in lending and the conflict in demand for certain kinds of materials necessitate this restriction.

The American Library Association has published a [this] manual explaining in detail the procedures which should be used in implementing the principles of this code. Libraries requesting materials on interlibrary loan are expected to have copies of this manual and to abide by its recommendations.

The present interlibrary loan system may be radically changed by less conventional methods of transmission of materials, such as telefacsimile and computer networks. Until such methods have gained widespread acceptance, their use must be based on special agreements among libraries.

THE CODE

I. *Definition*

Interlibrary loans are transactions in which library materials are made available by one library to another for the use of an individual; for the purposes of this code they include the provision of copies as substitutes for loans of the original materials.

---

[1]See chapter 2.

1

"by one library to another"—Individuals may not make direct requests for loans, but must ask their own library to make the request for them.

"for the use of an individual"—Each request should state the name and status of the individual for whom the request is made. The loan is for the exclusive use of that individual. If the item is to be used by more than one individual, such as a research team, this fact should be clearly indicated on the request. Music, play scripts, and other materials should not be borrowed for public performance.

"copies as substitutes"—See chapter 5.

II. *Purpose*

The purpose of interlibrary loans is to make available, for *research,* materials not owned by a given library, in the belief that the furtherance of knowledge is in the general interest. Interlibrary loan service supplements a library's resources by making available, for the use of an individual, materials from other libraries not owned by the borrowing library.

"for research"—Generally, in interpreting whether material is requested for research, the key is "furtherance of knowledge" that will ultimately be available in some form to a relevant public.

III. *Responsibility of Borrowing Libraries*

1. It is assumed that each library will provide the resources to meet the study, instructional, informational, and normal research needs of its users, and that requests for materials from another library will be limited to unusual items which the library does not own and cannot readily obtain at moderate cost. Requests for individuals with academic affiliations should be limited to those materials needed for faculty and staff research, and the thesis and dissertation research of graduate students.

"cannot readily obtain"—In-print items should be purchased or a photocopy or microfilm obtained.

"at moderate cost"—This will vary according to circumstances and to the budget and resources of the borrowing library.

2. Thesis topics should be selected according to the resources on hand and should not require extensive borrowing from other libraries. If an individual needs to use a large number of items located in another library, he should make arrangements to use them at that library.

"he should make arrangements to use them at that library"—Students should be warned and faculty alerted to the need to obtain written permission in ad-

vance, preferably before the thesis topic is submitted for approval, and the user should be prepared to pay a research fee for the use of the material.

3. The borrowing library should screen carefully all applications for loans and should reject those which do not conform to this code.

IV. *Responsibility of Lending Libraries*

1. In the interests of furthering research it is desirable that lending libraries interpret as generously as possible their own lending policies, with due consideration to the interests of their primary clientele.

"interpret as generously as possible"—Libraries having the policy of lending materials included in section V.2 below (such as serials, microfilm dissertations. and genealogical materials) should not interpret this code to mean that such lending should be discontinued. All libraries should interpret their policies as generously as possible and be willing to make exceptions.

2. A lending library has the responsibility of informing any borrowing library of its apparent failure to follow the provisions of this code.

"informing . . . of its apparent failure"—See pages 46 and 78.

V. *Scope*

1. Any type of library material needed for the purpose of research may be requested on loan or in photocopy from another library. The lending library has the privilege of deciding in each case whether a particular item should or should not be provided, and whether the original or a copy should be sent.

2. Libraries should not ordinarily ask, however, to borrow the following types of materials:
   a. U.S. books in print of moderate cost
   b. Serials, when the particular item needed can be copied at moderate cost
   c. Rare materials, including manuscripts
   d. Basic reference materials
   e. Genealogical, heraldic and similar materials
   f. Bulky or fragile materials which are difficult and expensive to pack (*e.g.* newspapers)
   g. Typescript doctoral dissertations, when fully reproduced in microfilm and readily available.

"not ordinarily ask"—See also section IV.1 above. If the borrowing librarian

feels that extenuating circumstances justify requesting the loan, these circumstances should be explained, as indicated on page 27.

"U.S. books in print of moderate cost"—See section III.1 above.

"Serials, when the particular item needed can be copied at moderate cost"— If the text has illustrations that will not reproduce well, and the special need of the borrower requires the original, this fact should be indicated on the request.

"dissertations, when fully reproduced in microfilm and readily available"—See chapter 8. Some universities that film their own dissertations may omit maps, drawings, or other large material that was included in the original, unlike University Microfilms which always includes them. If a microfilm contains such omissions, a special annotated request to borrow might be justified, although it ought to be realized that the owning library may not be able to lend, especially if it has only one copy.

VI. *Expenses*

1. The borrowing library assumes the responsibility for all costs charged by the lending library, including transportation, insurance, copying, and any service charges. If the charges are more than nominal, and are not authorized beforehand by the borrowing library, the lending library should inform the requesting library and ask for authorization to proceed with the transaction. Borrowing libraries should try to anticipate charges, such as for copies, and authorize them on the original request.

"anticipate charges"—Borrowing libraries should own and consult the *Directory of Institutional Photocopying Services (Including Selected Interlibrary Loan Policies),* compiled by Cosby Brinkley, which will assist them in estimating photocopy charges.

2. It is recommended that in the interests of efficiency the lending library absorb costs which are nominal, such as for postage.

VII. *Conditions of Loans*

1. The safety of borrowed materials is the responsibility of the borrowing library. In case of loss or damage the borrowing library is obligated to meet all costs of repair or replacement, in accordance with the preferences of the lending library.

2. The borrowing library is bound by any limitations on use imposed by the lending library. It is recommended to lending libraries that any limitations (such as "for use in library only") be based on the physical condition or the bibliographic character of the particular item rather than be imposed on all materials lent.

"limitations on use"—This includes restrictions to use within the library building, restrictions on reproduction, signing by the individual borrower of a "use sheet" in front of thesis, etc. See pages 40–41.

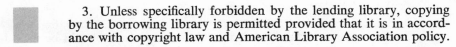

3. Unless specifically forbidden by the lending library, copying by the borrowing library is permitted provided that it is in accordance with copyright law and American Library Association policy.

"Unless specifically forbidden by the lending library"—The lending library should specify on the Interlibrary Loan Request form "Copying not permitted" for any item that it wishes to deny permission to photocopy, whether because of condition or other reasons.

"copyright law and American Library Association policy"—See chapter 5.

VIII. *Placement of Requests*

1. Libraries should exhaust local resources and make an effort to locate copies through the use of bibliographical tools, union lists, and union catalogs. Requests should be made to one of the nearer institutions known to possess the desired material. Care should be taken, however, to avoid concentrating requests on a few libraries.

"make an effort to locate copies"—See pages 24–25, 52–53, and 98–104.

2. In the absence of special agreements, requests should normally be placed by mail using the standard ALA forms, or by teletype using a format based on the ALA interlibrary loan form. When an urgent request is made by telephone, this initial request should be immediately followed by the confirming ALA form.

"form"—See pages 26–38 for ILL form and 56–60 for teletype form.

IX. *Form of Request*

1. Materials requested must be described completely and accurately following accepted bibliographic practice.

See pages 22–23 and 25–37.

2. Items requested should be verified and sources of verification given, and for this purpose borrowing libraries should have access to basic bibliographic tools. When the item requested cannot be verified, the statement "Cannot verify" should be included with complete information on the original source of reference. If this provision is disregarded and the bibliographic data appear to be incorrect, the request may be returned unfilled without special effort to identify the reference.

See pages 20–22 and 45–46.

3. The name and status (position or other identifying information) of the individual for whom the material is being requested should be included on the request form.

See section III.1 above and page 27.

4. A standard ALA interlibrary loan form should be used for each item requested (or an ALA photoduplication order form, when it is known that copies will be supplied and payment required).

5. All correspondence and shipments should be conspicuously labeled "Interlibrary Loan."

See also section VIII.2 above and pages 26–38 for ALA interlibrary loan form, appendix A for photoduplication form, and pages 56–60 for teletype form. For sample of parcel labels, see appendix B.

X. *Duration of Loan*

1. Unless otherwise specified by the lending library, the duration of loan is normally calculated to mean the period of time the item may remain with the borrowing library, disregarding the time spent in transit.

"Unless otherwise specified"—If the lending library wants to be sure that the item is returned to it by a specific date, that date should be stated on the form. To clarify this, some libraries so indicate, for example: "Due back at NjParB by Mr 15, needed for reserve."

2. The borrowing library should ask for renewal only in unusual circumstances, and a second renewal should never be asked for without a specific explanation. The renewal request should be sent in time to reach the lending library on or before the date due. The lending library should respond to renewal requests promptly; if it does not, it will be assumed that renewal for the same length as the original loan period is granted.

3. Material on loan is subject to recall at any time and the borrowing library should comply promptly.

4. The loan period specified by the lending library should be appropriate to the type of material.

"loan period"—For example, if the lending library specifies "four weeks" and sends the item on February 22, the borrowing library receiving it on March 1 should mail it back no later than March 28.

XI. *Notification and Acknowledgment*

1. The lending library is expected to notify the requesting library promptly whether or not the material is being sent; if the material cannot be supplied, the lending library should state the reason.

"state the reason"—See the Not Sent Because section of the ALA Interlibrary Loan Request form. In addition to the reasons specified there is space provided for sending other information. Lending libraries are urged to make a special effort to locate materials that the borrowing library has indicated (see pages 24–25, 46–47) have been located through union lists or the Union Catalog Division of the Library of Congress; if the material is not found, the lending library should indicate the reason for the inability to fill the request. Many universities also make a special effort to trace requests for their theses and dissertations. If the lending library owns some of a serial title, but not the issue requested, it should indicate, "lacks v. 57."

2. Except in the case of very valuable shipments, no acknowledgment of receipt is necessary. If there is undue delay in receipt, however, the receiving library has a responsibility to notify the lending library so that a search may be initiated promptly.

"valuable shipments"—If the lending library wishes the borrowing library to acknowledge receipt of the item, it should be noted on form B report.

"undue delay in receipt"—This will differ with the distance the material is to be sent, but it is usually interpreted as approximately ten days beyond expected date of arrival.

XII. *Violation of Code*

Continued disregard of any of the provisions of this code is sufficient reason for suspension of borrowing privileges.

As indicated in section IV.2 above, the lending library is responsible for informing the borrowing library of its apparent failure to follow the provisions of this code. If the borrowing library continues to disregard these provisions after notification, the lending library may decline to lend. (See also appendix E.)

2/Model Interlibrary Loan Code

for Regional, State, Local, or Other Special Groups of Libraries, Annotated

COMMENTS ON ADAPTING THE MODEL CODE

The text of the model code presented here is intended to include as many provisions as possible which would be applicable to a variety of situations. This explains what on a careful analysis might seem to be ambiguous or contradictory statements. Groups of libraries planning to use the model code must realize that it cannot be adopted without changes which will reflect the special circumstances of particular areas.

It should be further understood that the Interlibrary Loan Committee of the ALA Reference Services Division does not intend to suggest that the solutions offered here are the only possible ones.

It is important that all libraries participate in the preliminary discussions and formulation of a local code. No library should be expected to subscribe automatically, or without reservations, to a code because it happens to be located in a given geographical area or to belong to a particular group of libraries.

Matters not spelled out in this model code (for example, screening and routing procedures, charges for photocopying, special contractual agreements, designated resource libraries) should be explicitly stated in detail when a given group of libraries agrees upon a code.

There should be some provisions for revisions in the light of changing conditions and needs. The local code and a manual for procedures should be widely distributed.

The comments above describe the context in which it is intended that this local code be accepted, adopted, and followed by a group of libraries. It is important that they be read and understood before proceeding to interpret the code itself. Where the local code model continues to follow the language of the national code, referral should be made to the interpretation of the national code in chapter 1 of this manual. Sections thus self-explanatory are not commented upon in this chapter. Similarly, comment indicative of restrictions under the national code may well be considered for writing into the local code, *not as restrictions, but as liberalized provisions.*

INTRODUCTION

This code is a voluntary agreement adopted by _____ on _____ to govern interlibrary lending among libraries [in the _____ region, in the state of _____, in the metropolitan area of _____, or _____ group of _____ libraries]. Although correlated with the ALA National Interlibrary Loan Code, 1968 (adopted by the Reference Services Division, acting for the American Library Association on June 27, 1968) this local code is intended to promote a more liberalized interlibrary loan policy among the libraries adopting it. It is based on the premise that lending among libraries for the use of an individual [in the _____ region, in the state of _____, etc.] is in the public interest and should be encouraged. However, liberal interlibrary lending should be no substitute for the development of adequate collections based on the needs of the service areas represented in libraries and library systems.

This code may be further expanded or modified to meet the particular interests of participating libraries. . . .

"a voluntary agreement"—Once the provisions have been agreed upon, it is expected that the participants will honor the local code as established.

"a more liberalized interlibrary loan policy"—The heart of the local code is this statement. Specific examples of a more generous interlibrary loan practice are included in the model; others may be stipulated and added to the model as agreed upon.

"in the public interest"—The group of libraries becoming signatory to the code will recognize the patron interests of the area or group of libraries involved and will seek to meet those interests in the adoption of the local code.

"interlibrary lending should be no substitute for . . . adequate collections based on the needs of the service areas represented"—A fitting corollary to the adoption of the code could be the development of an area or local acquisitions policy; however, in its absence, each local library or library system should define its collection-building intentions and should use interlibrary loan records as keys to recognition of needs, buying when recurrent demand warrants.

See also section IV, Responsibility of Borrowing Libraries.

THE CODE

I. *Definition*

1. Interlibrary loans are transactions in which library materials are made available by one library to another; for the purposes of this code they also include the provision of copies as substitutes for loans of the original materials.

II. *Purpose*

1. Since it is increasingly evident that it is impossible for any one library to be self-sufficient, and in the belief that the furtherance of knowledge is in the general interest, interlibrary borrowing and lending is regarded by the libraries subscribing to this agreement as essential to library service.

"interlibrary borrowing and lending is . . . essential to library service"— Agreement among the parties to this code signifies acceptance of this principle, within the provisions contained therein, and with recognition of the factor of interdependence among all types of libraries represented.

III. *Responsibility of Lending Libraries*

1. Lending libraries have the responsibility of informing borrowing libraries of any failure to observe the provisions of this code, and if necessary may invoke the provisions stated in Sec. XII.

2. Lending libraries will practice as liberal and unrestrictive a policy as is possible in interlibrary loans, with due consideration to the interests of their primary clientele.

"as liberal and unrestrictive a policy as . . . possible"—The policy is spelled out further in section V, Scope. It may be extended to other kinds of materials and types of libraries. Thus it might be possible to include all types of libraries *and their borrowers* without restriction. It might also extend to materials not allowable under the national code, e.g., material for class use, nonbook materials, filmstrips and slides, or recordings.

IV. *Responsibility of Borrowing Libraries*

1. It is recognized that interlibrary lending does not relieve any library of the responsibility of developing its own collection. Each library will provide the resources to meet the ordinary study, educational, instructional, informational, and research needs of its users. Requests to borrow from other libraries will be limited to those items which the library might not be expected to own. No library should depend upon another to supply the normal needs of its clientele except under special agreement for such service.

"ordinary study, educational, instructional, informational, and research needs" —Each library will and should define these according to the need of its community and of the clientele for which it is responsible. A clear understanding of these needs will facilitate the satisfactory working of this agreement and will allow each individual library to function in interlibrary lending in a proper manner.

"special agreement"—Such agreements are entirely possible; however, it should be recognized that their provisions may be outside the terms of the

local code. They could be supplemental to and needful of temporary or permanent arrangements, e.g., the loan of bulk materials for a specific purpose—such as a Head Start class—or a regularly renewable contract between a public library and a school district. It should be clearly understood that such agreements may not necessarily be allowable under a broader local code, and that interlibrary lending as applicable in the local code may not pertain.

> 2. Borrowing libraries will make every effort to exhaust their own resources before resorting to interlibrary loans.

> 3. Borrowing libraries will screen carefully all applications for loans, rejecting those which do not conform to this code. (See also Art. VII, Conditions of Loans; Art. IX, Form of Request.)

V. *Scope*

> 1. Any type of library material needed for the purposes of study, instruction, information, or research may be requested on loan or in photocopy from another library. The lending library has the privilege of deciding in each case whether a *particular* item should or should not be provided, and whether the original or a copy should be sent. These decisions may be determined by the nature of the material or its physical condition, the degree of active demand for the material requested [or other reasons specifically indicated in this agreement].

"the purposes of study, instruction, information, or research"—This is a liberalizing statement which extends traditional interlibrary lending; however, adequate protection exists for the lending library. Under the terms of the local code, it is expected that the average patron's need for informational materials, as well as the undergraduate or elementary or secondary school student's need for materials not normally found in his school library, might be met. Similarly, specific restrictions should be written into the local code, yet at the same time, items discouraged in the national code, such as some of those listed in section I.1 (chapter 1), may be indicated as lendable in a local code. These items could include serials, microfilm, paperbacks, genealogy, or local history.

> 2. Under the terms of this agreement it is permissible to request on interlibrary loan:
>
> a. Materials collected in specialized subject fields and in special nonrestricted collections;
>
> b. Materials collected under special acquisition agreements;
>
> c. Materials bought under special grant or other programs intended to promote economical use of the total resources of the area;
>
> d. Reference materials whenever lending might not hinder the service of the lending library.

Certain provisions more generous than the national code are indicated in this section and include those named.

"collected under special acquisitions agreements"—For example, specific reference collections or titles; microforms; newspapers; foreign-language materials.

"bought under special grant or other programs"—Under several of the federal acts pertaining to library cooperation or to the purchase of library materials—e.g., LSCA Title I, Higher Education Act Title II C, and under some state grant programs—materials bought may be purchased for use in library systems or among groups of libraries. Such materials may well be singled out as suitable to and available for interlibrary lending.

3. Under the terms of this agreement, borrowing libraries will not ordinarily request:
   a. Books in current and/or recurring demand;
   b. Bulky or fragile materials;
   c. Rare materials;
   d. A large number of titles for one person at any one time;
   e. Duplicates of titles already owned;
   f. Materials which can be copied cheaply;
   g. Materials for class, reserve, or other group use.

Among the materials, unless otherwise stipulated in the local code, which should *not* be borrowed in most circumstances, particular attention should focus on these:

"Books in current and/or recurring demand"—This is to say that the gauge of demand is to be not only the responsibility of the lender to deny, but the responsibility of the borrower *not to ask*. Best sellers, newly published materials of popular and highly current interest, and titles which are asked for day after day come in this category. The borrowing library should consider these for possible purchase or should acquire these by subscription to plans which serve to satisfy current and popular needs. In some systems special agreements may be required which will allow the loan of such materials outside the purview of this code.

"A large number of titles for one person"—This is almost self-explanatory. The local code may wish to define more specifically; however, usually common sense will dictate the use of this statement.

"Duplicates of titles"—Normal expectation considers that added purchase is the answer or, if not feasible, that a reserve policy be established in the borrowing library and fully explained to patrons. Another library should not be

expected to lend a title already in the borrowing library, except in unusual circumstances. Nor should a lending library be requested to put such a title on a reserve status for interlibrary lending purposes.

"class, reserve, or other group use"—If this is a part of the agreement, it should be so interpreted for those libraries seeking to borrow for patrons for such purposes. Under certain conditions, and among certain groups of libraries, agreement may be stipulated in a local code in order to allow use of interlibrary loan for these purposes on justifiable occasions.

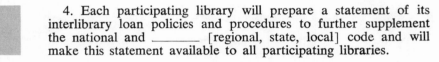

4. Each participating library will prepare a statement of its interlibrary loan policies and procedures to further supplement the national and _____ [regional, state, local] code and will make this statement available to all participating libraries.

This section is suggested as a logical supplement to this local code. Individual statements of policy from participating libraries may not merely serve as a basis for mutual agreement in the development of the code, they may well suffice to prevent misunderstanding of its application.

VI. *Expenses*

1. The borrowing library should be prepared to assume any costs charged by the lending library as agreed upon in this code. If the charges are more than nominal, and not authorized beforehand by the borrowing library, the lending library will inform the requesting library and obtain authorization to proceed with the transaction. Borrowing libraries should attempt to anticipate charges and authorize them on the initial request.

Such costs as postage, photocopying, or insurance may be absorbed by mutual understanding within specified limits and conditions.

2. In the interests of efficiency the lending library may agree to absorb nominal costs for:

a. Postage;

b. Photocopying;

c. Insurance.

Mutual understanding may agree to absorption of such costs as postage, photocopying, or insurance, within specified limits and conditions.

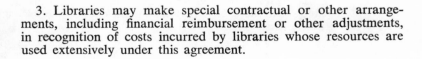

3. Libraries may make special contractual or other arrangements, including financial reimbursement or other adjustments, in recognition of costs incurred by libraries whose resources are used extensively under this agreement.

"special contractual or other arrangements"—When certain libraries are recognized as bearing major burdens for a group or in an area, methods may be developed for the provision of some reimbursement to them. The code may write in an arrangement for a credit transfer based on periodic settlement of accounts. State plans may recognize and reimburse designated resource libraries expected to provide an amount of interlibrary loan service which is clearly extensive.

See also sections V and VIII.1.

VII. *Conditions of Loans*

1. The borrowing library will honor any limitations on use imposed by the lending library.

2. Unless specifically forbidden by the lending library, it is assumed that copying is permitted, provided that it is in accordance with copyright law and ALA policy and further, provided no damage to the original volume will result.

3. The borrowing library is responsible for returning loans promptly and in good condition.

4. The safety of borrowed materials is the responsibility of the borrowing library. The borrowing library will meet all costs of repair or replacement in accordance with the preferences of the lending library.

VIII. *Placement of Requests*

1. Special arrangements for lending of materials by designated resource libraries may be made within the context of this agreement. Requests should be routed through such established channels as may be agreed upon by libraries participating in a local, state, or regional plan for library service.

"Special arrangements"—Resource libraries may be named in this code either within the structure of library systems or by type of library. The channels or routes to their services may be indicated pursuant to library plans; such arrangements may become part of a local code. Agreement to honor the named channels will expedite access to materials in interlibrary lending and will distribute the load of lending in a much more equable manner.

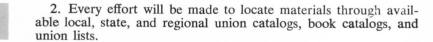

2. Every effort will be made to locate materials through available local, state, and regional union catalogs, book catalogs, and union lists.

"available local, state, and regional union catalogs," etc.—These are tools

serving as recognized assets to interlibrary lending. They will improve access and will aid in the elimination of fruitless or random searching for materials. Where they exist, they should be so recognized in the local code.

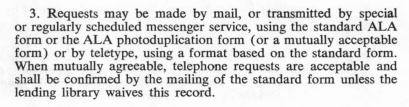

> 3. Requests may be made by mail, or transmitted by special or regularly scheduled messenger service, using the standard ALA form or the ALA photoduplication form (or a mutually acceptable form) or by teletype, using a format based on the standard form. When mutually agreeable, telephone requests are acceptable and shall be confirmed by the mailing of the standard form unless the lending library waives this record.

Local codes are logical vehicles for expediting interlibrary lending. Where messenger services or courier routes are operative, the local code may want to recognize their existence, and to include them as proper routes of access. By the same token, methods of transmittal other than the standard ALA form, provided the necessary elements of information are formated, are acceptable provisions in a local code. Teletype systems may be standardized by their recognition in a local code.

> 4. No library will lend directly to an individual on an interlibrary loan basis, except by mutual agreement between the borrowing and the lending libraries.

IX. *Form of Request*

> 1. Materials requested must be described as completely and accurately as possible following accepted bibliographic practice.

"accepted bibliographic practice"—This is dealt with specifically in chapter 3 and should be read carefully. Each signatory to a local agreement should be prepared to honor this requirement to the best of its ability unless otherwise specified.

> 2. All items requested shall be verified in standard bibliographic tools and sources of verification cited. When the item requested cannot be verified, the statement "cannot verify" shall be indicated, and complete information as to source of reference furnished.

"standard bibliographic tools"—Depending upon the type of library included in the agreement, and perhaps depending upon agreed-upon channels—as in a statewide or regional system, it will be expected that each library own and use basic bibliographic tools in the verification of its interlibrary loan requests. Some local codes may wish to indicate the minimum tools, use of which would be expected.

"sources of verification"—If standard tools do not serve to verify a requested item, the source of verification may be important. Effort should be made to discover it at the time the individual patron requests the loan, e.g., is it to be found in a footnote, abstract, bibliography? The local code may choose to make such a requirement dependent upon the filling of a request by the lending institution.

3. If verification is disregarded, or the bibliographic data is incorrect, and unless special agreement otherwise provides, the lending library may return the request unfilled without special effort to identify the reference.

4. The name and status (position or other identifying information) of the individual for whom the material is being requested shall appear on the request form.

5. All requests and shipments shall be conspicuously labeled "Interlibrary Loan."

X. *Duration of Loan*

1. Unless otherwise specified by the lending library, the duration of the loan shall be calculated as the time the item is to be in the borrowing library, disregarding the time spent in transit. The period of loan shall be that ordinarily extended by the lending library.

Development of a local code may spell out the variances in loan periods and may provide a mean standard for interlibrary lending; if it does not, the lending library will indicate and expect its loan period to be honored.

2. Renewal requests shall be kept to a minimum. The renewal request shall be sent in time to reach the lending library before the due date. The lending library should respond to renewal requests promptly; if it does not, it will be assumed that renewal for the same period as the original loan is granted.

This is self-explanatory. Renewals should be sought rarely and with good reason.

3. The loan period specified by the lending library should be appropriate to the type of material.

4. The borrowing library is responsible for returning interlibrary loans promptly and in good condition.

5. Material on loan is subject to recall at any time and the borrowing library shall comply promptly.

XI. *Notification and Acknowledgement*

1. The lending library shall notify the borrowing library promptly whether or not the material is being sent; if the material cannot be supplied, the lending library shall state the reason.

2. Except in the case of very valuable shipments, no acknowledgement of receipt is necessary. If there is undue delay in receipt of shipments, the borrowing library shall notify the lending library so that a search may be initiated.

XII. *Violation of the Code*

1. Continued disregard of the provisions of this code shall be sufficient reason for suspension of borrowing privileges.

3/Instructions for Borrowing Libraries

SUPPLIES

Minimum supplies needed:

ALA Interlibrary Loan Request forms, as revised 1968 (see figure 1). These forms are available from most library supply houses.[1] It is recommended that the name and full address of the borrowing library be imprinted for clarity and to prevent inadvertent reversal of borrowing and lending library addresses.

3x5 self-addressed gummed return shipping labels (see appendix B). These are also available from library supply houses.

Adequate packing supplies for protecting the item for its safe return (see pages 41 and 48).

Policy statements of libraries frequently borrowed from.

Additional supplies recommended:

Workslip forms for readers to enter their request, address, etc. (For suggested sample, see page 20 and appendix C.) These will probably be mimeographed or printed by each borrowing library, since requirements may differ.

3x5 gummed shipping labels with address space blank but with library's return address. These are available from library supply houses and are useful for many library purposes other than interlibrary loan (see appendix B).

Forms for requesting locations from the Union Catalog Division of the Library of Congress (see figure 18 and chapter 6).

Standard window envelopes.

ALA photoduplication order forms (see appendix A).

---

[1]For sample list of library supply houses, see *Library Journal* annual issue.

INSTRUCTIONS

    1. Follow the Interlibrary Loan Code.

The "National Interlibrary Loan Code, 1968" has been reproduced in its entirety in chapter 1 of this manual, with annotations interpreting specific sections. The national code should be followed whenever requests are made to research libraries, regardless of proximity, and to all other libraries unless a local or special code has been mutually agreed upon. A copy of the recommended model state, local, or regional code is included in chapter 2. Libraries should obtain copies of their local code from their state or regional library, or from the local sponsoring library association. Every librarian who requests loans should be familiar with the provisions of these codes.

    2. Instruct your readers about interlibrary loan.

Most readers do not know what to expect of interlibrary loan, what materials it is appropriate to request, the amount of time required, and the common restrictions on use and photoduplication. Some libraries find it helpful to have to distribute to their readers a prepared statement, usually summarizing relevant sections of the code. (See appendix J for example.)

Train your readers, of all levels of sophistication, to take careful notes of the full citation and source of reference for items in their bibliographies, and to work with you in the systematic verification of these references. Many faculty members and highly competent research personnel are not aware of the need to verify or of the usefulness of the *Union List of Serials, New Serial Titles,* and the *National Union Catalog* in verification and location. If the librarian and the reader work together, each benefits from the knowledge of the other.

Lending libraries vary widely in what they may be willing to lend and to what categories of readers. Some lending libraries are willing to lend journals, rare books, and even reference books, if the need and purpose are significant, the borrower qualified, and the loan will neither endanger the material nor deprive the lending library's own readers. Many other libraries are much more restrictive in their policies. This variance should be explained to readers.

Make it clear to your readers that interlibrary loan is a library-to-library transaction, and that an individual's direct request to borrow will not be honored, although orders for photocopy, if prepaid, can sometimes be sent by an individual, if he so desires.

It is helpful, especially when working with students and faculty, to explain that at least two weeks should ordinarily be allowed for the arrival of loans by mail, that many lending libraries will not grant renewals, and that readers should plan their work in such a way that they will be able to work intensively on the borrowed material when it arrives. Students and their faculty advisers should be sternly warned of the hazards of selecting thesis topics for which essential materials must be borrowed from other libraries. Librarians talking with seminar and dissertation groups should stress this point.

3. Screen requests carefully. Obtain as much information as possible from the reader.

It is the responsibility of the librarian in the borrowing library to query the reader before accepting the request and to screen the request to determine whether the restrictions set forth in the code are met, particularly with regard to:

a. Purpose (see code, section II, page 2)
b. Status of reader (see code, section III, pages 2–3)
c. Type of material (see code, section V, pages 3–4).

Know your local code. It is likely that state, county, and regional libraries in your area may be far more liberal in lending practice than large research libraries; for example, most state and public libraries will borrow and lend for private study, and for undergraduate and even high school work; they will usually lend materials in print and some of them will lend serials and genealogical materials.

If the item is something that can only be obtained from a research library, and either the purpose or status of readers is such that a *loan* request is contrary to the national code, the borrowing library should try to make funds available to purchase a copy of the original or a photocopy.

Find out where the reader originally learned about the item: whether from a footnote or bibliography, from a review or trade catalog, or from another person. Train him to note fully where citations were found; examination of the original citation may delimit the item by date, correct misspelling, prevent attribution of theses to wrong universities, detect parts of series, etc.

Most libraries find it helpful to provide a workslip form on which the reader records as completely as he can the bibliographic information for the item wanted, the source of reference, and his own name, status, address, and telephone number. The librarian, while working with the reader, records his purpose and notes the verification sources searched, with volume and page where found, checks the accuracy of the bibliographic citation and completes it when necessary, and notes the libraries which union lists report own the item. Separate workslip forms for serial and nonserial requests are less confusing and result in fewer omissions than a combined form. Since the needs of borrowing libraries differ, each will probably wish to design and mimeograph its own workslips, but a checklist of items to consider for inclusion and some sample forms are given in appendix C. The Interlibrary Loan Request form is filled in from the workslip.

4. Verify citations.

Items wanted on interlibrary loan should be verified and the verification source noted in full, before the Interlibrary Loan Request form is typed.

To verify a citation means to:

a. Confirm or establish the existence of the item by locating it in an authoritative bibliography, preferably in the published catalog of a major library, or in a standard indexing source, such as *Chemical Abstracts, Cumulative Book Index, National Union Catalog, New Serial Titles, Newspapers on Microfilm, Readers' Guide to Periodical Literature, Union List of Serials.*

b. Supply and check the exactness of all components of the standard bibliographic citation. These requirements are discussed in detail on pages 22–23 and 29–37.

c. Use as a main entry the Library of Congress entry or the form found in standard American union lists. The Library of Congress entry will facilitate the lending library's finding the item in its catalog. If it is not possible to supply this entry, the citation should be checked in several different appropriate sources, and the variations in the form of the main entry should be noted.

The borrowing librarian should enter on the workslip the complete bibliographic citation and the full citation to the source of verification, including volume, series, and date where appropriate, with the page on which the verification was found. (For example, see figures 1–8, 10–14.)

If the verification source is included in the "Standard Abbreviations of Sources of Verification," appendix N, abbreviate it precisely as given in that list. Verification sources not included in the standard list should be cited in full. Remember that verification sources and abbreviations familiar to the borrowing librarian may not be known to the librarian attempting to fill the request.

In requests for periodical articles, both the title of the periodical and the article wanted should be verified, and both sources of verification given. For example: NST (1950-60) 2:783; MLA 73:236. It is not sufficient merely to verify the title of the journal since the reader may have the volume or year wrong or even the wrong journal. If it is not possible to verify the periodical article, the source of reference for the article should be given in full.

If the item is not readily verified by the borrowing librarian, the source of reference given by the reader should be carefully checked to see if the information was correctly copied, or if the source gives additional information in some footnote or bibliography to help identify the citation. If the date of the source of reference is known, the librarian at least knows that the wanted item probably existed or was in progress before that date. Footnotes often refer to research still in progress, and the reader requesting the item may not notice that the item was not yet published.[2]

---

[2]For additional suggestions on verification procedures, see Margaret Hutchins, *Introduction to Reference Work* (Chicago: American Library Assn., 1944), p.41–51,

Series notes are especially important. A library may own the series without having analyzed it in its catalog, and this discovery may lead the librarian and the reader to the item, making an interlibrary loan unnecessary. Or the *Union List of Serials* may provide locations for the series. Include the series note on the Interlibrary Loan Request form, since the lending library's entry may vary.

Do not overlook the possibility that the item may have been reprinted in a collection which you already own.

After verifying the item, search your own card catalog and outstanding order files, to be sure you do not have the item or have it on order.

Libraries of all types and sizes have an obligation to build their own bibliographic collections and to supplement them through established channels. Libraries with limited bibliographic resources should make standing arrangements with nearby libraries that own major bibliographies, especially those titles listed on page 21, to assist them in verifying and locating titles before making requests. For public libraries, school libraries, and many special libraries, requests will be channeled through county and regional libraries to the state library if necessary.

If a library, after thorough search, is unable to verify a citation, it should send as much information as possible to the library with whom it has made verification and location arrangements. This information should include:

a. Citation, as fully as is known
b. Full citation to the source of reference, including full author, title, publisher, place, and date, and page on which the citation appears
c. A list of the sources searched.

Most large libraries are more willing to search if there is clear indication that the borrowing library has made every effort to use its own resources. The fuller the information given the verifying library, the greater the chance that it will be able to identify and locate the item. In cases where the citation is very complex, has series notes, is in a foreign language, especially in a non-Roman alphabet, or is abbreviated, photocopy the page and send it stapled to the request.

5. Provide accurate and complete bibliographic citations.

190–91, pass. See also George Lowy, *Searcher's Manual* (Hamden, Conn.: Shoe String Press, 1965) and the *Anglo-American Cataloging Rules* (Chicago: American Library Assn., 1967).

The distinction between verification sources and sources of reference is not always precise. Bibliographies vary in reliability and in the form of entry used for many titles. Many reference books, such as encyclopedias and bibliographical dictionaries, would, in the strict sense of the term, be considered sources of reference, rather than sources of verification. "Source of reference" as used on the ALA Interlibrary Loan Request form refers to the textbook, dissertation, periodical article, etc., in which the reader originally found the citation.

Copy the citation found in the verification source precisely and in full. Samples of citations with verification sources, by type of material requested, are given on pages 29–37.

Citations to books and other nonserial publications should include the author's full name, complete title, edition, place of publication, publisher, and date. The importance of including the date cannot be overemphasized; it is a great aid to the lending library in checking the card catalog and other bibliographies.

Citations to periodicals and other serials should give the name of the periodical in full, the volume and date, author and title of the article wanted, and the inclusive pagination.

When there are several journals with similar titles, include place of publication and sponsoring body to distinguish the one wanted. Place of publication should always be included for newspapers.

Use the Library of Congress, *Union List of Serials (ULS),* or *New Serial Titles (NST)* entry as given. However, if the periodical has changed title, the citation should be made under the title at the time of the article wanted, and the latest title should be noted in brackets.[3]

6. Do not use initials or abbreviations unless these initials or abbreviations are the actual title of the item.

If the title of the journal is a series of initials, it should be so cited, but spelled out in full in brackets, especially for scientific, technical, and foreign-language publications.

However, if a citation is abbreviated in the source of reference, and the borrowing library has no tools to determine what the abbreviation stands for, it is much better to send the request exactly as given than to guess (and guess wrong) what the abbreviation means.

As explained on page 22, series notes should always be given.

Remember that your requests will usually be checked, not by subject specialists who can guess or decipher what you mean, but by interlibrary loan librarians or clerical assistants who must find the entry in the general card catalog, which may contain millions of cards. Do not assume that because the title is familiar to you it is familiar to the librarian who will check the request. You are asking the lending library to do you a favor; if you make it as easy and as foolproof as possible, you are more likely to get what you want.

---

[3]Admittedly this is a controversial point. Some librarians advocate always citing under the name that appears in *ULS,* with the former name in parentheses. However, a journal may have gone through a variety of changes of name, mergers, separations, etc., and may appear in *ULS* in one form and *NST* in another. Therefore, citation under the name as it appeared in the issue wanted, with reference to other names, is less likely to cause confusion.

7. Find out before sending the request what library owns the item wanted.

Forty percent of the unfilled interlibrary loan requests, approximately 200,000 interlibrary loan requests a year, are not filled because the request was sent to a library that did not own the item.[4] Requests for materials that the lending library does not own take more staff time to handle in the lending library than requests for materials that it owns, since the librarian must verify the citation to be sure whether or not the item is owned. Requests sent to libraries that do not own the material also waste the time of the reader in the borrowing library, who waits impatiently, only to be told that the request aborted and another attempt must be made.

Determining in advance what library owns the item wanted will do more to increase the proportion of requests filled than any other preparation the borrowing librarian can make.

Although no union list or union catalog is always correct and up to date, the probability of obtaining an item from a lending library located through a standard union list is several times greater than the probability of getting the item if the request is sent without predetermining whether the lending library has the item. Major bibliographies that give locations of copies include:

> *National Union Catalog* (see especially *Register of Additional Locations*)
> *Union List of Serials*
> *New Serial Titles*
> *Newspapers on Microfilm*
> *Chemical Abstracts. List of Periodicals with Key to Library Files.*

Do not use these merely as verification sources; utilize fully and accurately their location symbols. Read carefully the section Location Information on page xviii of the first volume of the *National Union Catalog, Pre-1956 Imprints.*

Indicate on the Interlibrary Loan Request form that a union list or a union catalog listed that lending library as owning the item, or that location was obtained through the Union Catalog Division at the Library of Congress:

> Location from NUC 1958-62 41:440
> Location from ULS 1:356
> Location from DLC-UCD.

Since "NUC" (without underlining) is widely used as the published *National Union Catalog,* it is suggested that "NUC pre-1956" be used for the retrospective catalog now being published by Mansell, and that "DLC-UCD" be used when the card catalog at the Library of Congress in Washington is meant. Many

---

[4]Sarah Katharine Thomson, "General Interlibrary Loan Services in Major Academic Libraries in the United States" (D.L.S. diss., Columbia University, 1967; Ann Arbor, Mich.: University Microfilms, 1968), p.142–43, 159–61.

lending libraries will do more checking if the ILL form indicates that their library was listed as having the material requested.

Small libraries that do not have the *Union List of Serials, New Serial Titles,* or the *National Union Catalog* should make arrangements to check locations and citations with a nearby library that does have them or to route requests through channels established by the state library.

When the borrowing library, after exhausting local resources, union lists, published catalogs, or regional union catalogs, cannot determine what library owns the item wanted, it should route the request through channels to the regional reference library or to the state library for referral, according to the strength of the library and to the referral pattern developed in each state. If the item cannot be located in the region, the Union Catalog Division at the Library of Congress may be able to inform the borrowing library of the location of a copy. Detailed instructions for requesting locations from the Union Catalog Division are given in chapter 6 of this manual. See also pages 98–100.

8. Check the lending policy of the lending library.

You should request copies of the statement of services offered and the loan policy of your state library, major libraries in your area, and other libraries from which you borrow frequently. An up-to-date file of these, possibly with a card-file summary, should be maintained by the interlibrary loan librarian.

The new fourth edition of Cosby Brinkley's *Directory of Institutional Photo-copying Services* will contain the following items relating to interlibrary loan:

> NUC symbol _____
> Serials not lent if reference less than _____ pages
> Dissertations accepted between _____ (date) and _____
> (date) are available for loan
> Dissertations accepted by our university since _____ (date)
> have been microfilmed by:
> _____University Microfilms
> _____Ourselves
> TWX number, if loan or photocopy requests are so accepted,

It is obviously futile to place a request for a dissertation or serial if such loans are contrary to the policy of the lending library. Chapter 8 of this manual explains how to order microfilm copies of dissertations from University Microfilms.

9. Follow the directions on the interlibrary loan forms carefully and supply all relevant information.

Obtain a supply of the revised 1968 Interlibrary Loan Request forms, which are obtainable from most library supply houses. (See figure 1.) Never put more than one title on a single request form. Even requests for two articles from the

A

INTERLIBRARY LOAN REQUEST

According to the A.L.A. Interlibrary Loan Code

REQUEST

REPORTS: Checked by ☐

SENT BY: ☐ Library rate

Charges $ _____ Insured for $ _____

Date sent _____

DUE _____

RESTRICTIONS: ☐ For use in library only

☐ Copying not permitted

NOT SENT BECAUSE: ☐ In use

☐ Non circulating ☐ Not owned

Estimated Cost of: Microfilm _____ Hard copy _____

BORROWING LIBRARY RECORD:

Date received _____

Date returned _____

By ☐ Library rate

Postage enclosed $ _____ Insured for $ _____

RENEWALS: *(Request and report on sheet C)*

Requested on _____

Renewed to _____ (or period of renewal)

Remarks: Not available locally, (this edition only.)

Date of request: Feb. 15, 1969.

Call-No. _____

↑ **Borrowing Library**

Fill in left half of form including both library addresses in full

Fold here →

INTERLIBRARY LOAN LIBRARIAN
BERGEN COMMUNITY COLLEGE
400 PARAMUS ROAD
PARAMUS, NEW JERSEY 07652

For use of   John Smith, M.D.   Status Faculty   Dept. Nursing

Author (or periodical title, vol. and year)

→ Moore, Robert Albert

Title (with author & pages for periodical articles) (Incl. edition, place & date)   ☒ This edition only

Textbook of pathology.   2nd ed. Philadelphia, W. B. Saunders, 1951

Verified in (or source of reference)

CBI 1949–52, page 1290.   Location through DLC–UCD.

If non-circulating, please supply ☐ Microfilm ☐ Hard copy if cost does not exceed $ _____

⇒ **Lending Library**

Fill in pertinent items under REPORTS; return sheets B and C to borrowing library

National Library of Medicine
Interlibrary Loan
8600 Wisconsin Avenue
Bethesda, Maryland 20014

Note: The receiving library assumes responsibility for notification of non-receipt.

AUTHORIZED BY: *Jane Jones* _____ **Title** Jane Jones, Librarian
(FULL NAME)

Form rev. 1-68

No. 488 GAYLORD BROS. INC.

NCR paper

REGISTERED TRADEMARK OF THE NATIONAL CASH REGISTER COMPANY

Fig. 1. Interlibrary Loan Request form—book request

same volume should be sent on separate request forms, but they should be mailed clipped together. <u>All requests should be neatly typed.</u> If your forms contain carbons, do not remove them, and do not separate the parts from the stub at the left side.

The blank space at the top is intended for a variety of purposes:

    a. Serial number. If your library has the practice of numbering its interlibrary loan requests serially, this number should be placed uniformly in the upper left corner, above *Date of request.*

    b. Remarks. Use for special instructions or circumstances, or explanations, for example: "Not available locally"; "Our copy missing"; "Have tried NNC, NIC, NN"; "Article contains plates important to reader; can you please make exception and lend the volume?"; "Please send airmail special delivery; we will reimburse"; "Please see letter attached from Mr. Smith explaining special circumstances"; "Publisher out of stock"; "Borrower has used in your library."

Date of request.

Borrowing Library. Complete name and full postal address including zip code must be included on every form. Since each form may be handled as a separate transaction, this information must appear on every request submitted. Be careful not to reverse borrowing library and lending library addresses; imprinted forms prevent this reversal.

For use of . . . Status . . . Department . . . See national code sections I and III.1. Many major libraries require this information before materials will be lent. If the request is in behalf of a student, degree sought should be indicated, example, "M.S. candidate thesis." If the request is for a research team, that fact should be so indicated. Especially for theses and dissertations, the request should list all readers who wish to use the item.

Author

Title   See examples, figures 1–8, 10–14.

Verified in

If non-circulating, please supply ☐ *Microfilm* ☐ *Hard copy if cost does not exceed $*_____. See pages 38–40 and chapter 5.

Lending Library. Give full name and address of lending library, including zip code. Address requests, as appropriate, to the attention of "Photoduplication Service" or "Interlibrary Loan Service." Consult Brinkley's *Directory of Institutional Photocopying Services* for addresses. Time will be saved if requests for materials in divisional libraries that do their own

Author (or periodical title, vol. and year)

Hammond, Matthew Brown

Title (with author & pages for periodical articles) (Incl. edition, place & date) ☐ This edition only

The cotton industry; an essay in American Economic History. Part I. The cotton culture and the cotton trade. N.Y., Macmillan, 1897.(Publ. of the Amer. Econ. Assn.n.s.no.I)

Verified in (or source of reference)

LC Cat (-1942) 63:308; location from ULS I:214.

If non-circulating, please supply ☐ Microfilm ☐ Hard copy if cost does not exceed $_____

Fig. 2. Book request, showing part and series titles (ILL form)

direct lending or photocopying are sent directly to that division. These divisions are indicated in Brinkley.

Authorized by. The legible *signature* (not initials) and the title of the librarian or staff member authorized to request loans should always be included. It is required by some major lending libraries. The librarian who signs the request should check and revise the request to be sure that all information has been included and that the citation and verification are correct.

Also published as Chemische Reihe Bd. 10. Lehrbucher u. Monographien aus dem Gebiete der exacten Wissenschaften. **A**

Date of request: June 16, 1969

Call-No. REQUEST

**INTERLIBRARY LOAN LIBRARIAN
BERGEN COMMUNITY COLLEGE
400 PARAMUS ROAD
PARAMUS, NEW JERSEY 07652**

For use of   Prof. Smith   Status Chairman   Dept. Chem.

Author (or periodical title, vol. and year)

Simmons, Samuel William, ed.

Title (with author & pages for periodical articles) (Incl. edition, place & date) ☐ This edition only

Human and veterinary medicine. Basel, Birkhauser, 1959. (DDT: the insecticide Dichlorodiphenyltrichloroethane and its significance, v.2)

Verified in (or source of reference)   and located through:
NUC 1958-62 41:440

If non-circulating, please supply ☐ Microfilm ☐ Hard copy if cost does not exceed $_____

Fig. 3. Book request, one volume of a set (ILL form)

This Coupon will be accepted by the

CLEARINGHOUSE
FOR FEDERAL SCIENTIFIC AND TECHNICAL INFORMATION

in lieu of

65

cents

for the purchase
of one document
in microfiche form

EAC/CDC L 9744-B

INSTRUCTIONS:

1. Order document by ACCESSION/REPORT NUMBER ONLY. PRINT OR TYPE ACCESSION/REPORT NUMBER ON FRONT OF THIS CARD. If Accession/Report Number is unknown, provide document identification information, e.g., Author, Contract Number, Corporate Author, Title, below:

2. PRINT OR TYPE YOUR NAME AND ADDRESS CLEARLY ON FRONT. Be sure to include your ZIP CODE. This coupon will be returned to you as the address label with the document you order.

3. Submit ONE COUPON for EACH COPY of each document requested.

4. Do not fold, spindle, or otherwise mutilate this card.

5. Mail completed coupons to:

Department A
CLEARINGHOUSE
Springfield, Va. 22151

Fig. 9A. Coupon form for ordering reports from Clearinghouse (microfiche form)

EAC L 56098

Instructions:
1. If AD or PB number is unknown, provide document identification below:

SPONSOR'S SERIES #	CONTRACT OR GRANT # OF REPORT	DATE PUBLISHED
REPORT TITLE AND PERSONAL AUTHORS		
ORIGINATING ACTIVITY (GIVE SPECIFIC LABORATORY OR DIVISION AND LOCATION)		

2. IF A DDC CUSTOMER, furnish Contract Number and User Code information in spaces provided on front of card.
3. PRINT OR TYPE YOUR NAME, ADDRESS, INCLUDING ZIP CODE CLEARLY ON FRONT.
4. Submit ONE COUPON for EACH COPY of each document requested.
5. Do not fold, spindle, or otherwise mutilate this card.
6. Mail completed coupon to:

Department A
CLEARINGHOUSE
Springfield, Virginia 22151

This coupon will be accepted by the CLEARINGHOUSE for Federal Scientific and Technical Information in lieu of

$3.00

for the purchase of one document in paper copy form

Fig. 9B. Coupon form for ordering reports from Clearinghouse (paper-copy form)

such as the contract number, sponsoring federal agency, and author of the report, or cite the source of information, e.g., trade journal, etc.[6]

The Clearinghouse requires prepayment on all orders, either by rapid-service prepaid document coupons, available in books for either paper copy (HC) or microfiche (MF), deposit accounts, or check or money order.

PERIODICAL ARTICLE AND OTHER SERIAL REQUESTS

> *Author (or periodical title, volume and year):* Give the periodical title as listed in *Union List of Serials* or *New Serial Titles*. <u>Do not use abbreviations.</u> This takes much more time for the lending library to decipher. <u>Do not use initials unless the initials are actually the name of the journal.</u> If the name of the journal is a series of initials, the entry should follow that form, but be spelled out in full in brackets. If the serial has changed its name, the entry should be under the name it had at the time of the issue wanted, but with the latest name given in brackets (see page 23). If several serials have similar names, include the places of publication and the issuing body. This information is available from *ULS, NST,* and most of the standard indexes.
>
> Always give volume number and full date if available. Complete date is helpful, especially for recent numbers.

> *Title (with author & pages for periodical articles):* Give the author's name in full if possible. Some indexes do not give the full name in the subject listing, but will give full name in the author listing or in the author index. The title of the article should be given in full. Every attempt should be made to ascertain the full title. If this is not possible, describe the subject of the article as fully as possible. Give inclusive pagination.

> *Verified in (or source of reference):* Both the title of the journal and the individual article should be verified. Verify the title of the journal in standard lists such as *Union Lists of Serials, New Serial Titles,* or Ulrich's. Verify the article, author of the article, complete title, and inclusive pagination in standard bibliographies or indexing services. If the article appears in a journal to which no index is available, the source of reference for the article should be given in full.

---

[6]See their information pamphlet *Clearinghouse for Federal Scientific and Technical Information, a Guide to Its Products and Services* (Washington: Govt. Print. Off., 1968), available from the Clearinghouse, U.S. Dept. of Commerce, Springfield, Va. 22151.

For use of   Status   Dept.

Author (or periodical title, vol. and year)

American Microscopical Society. Transactions. v.87, Oct. 1968

Title (with author & pages for periodical articles) (Incl. edition, place & date)   ☐ This edition only

Larsen, J.R. "The neurosecretory cells of the brain of Aedes aegypti in relation to larval molt, metamorphosis and ovarian development." pages 395-410.

Verified in (or source of reference)

IM January, 1969, p. 498. located through ULS

If non-circulating, please supply ☐ Microfilm ☒ Hard copy if cost does not exceed $ 3.00

Fig. 10. Periodical article request (ILL form)

Author (or periodical title, vol. and year)

Mississippi Valley Historical Review [title changed to Journal of American History] v.35, Dec. 1948

Title (with author & pages for periodical articles) (Incl. edition, place & date)   ☐ This edition only

Kramer, Frank R. "Effect of the Civil War on the public health movement." pages 449-462

Verified in (or source of reference) and located through ULS 3:2697

article verified in Int.I. 11:909

If non-circulating, please supply ☐ Microfilm ☒ Hard copy if cost does not exceed $ 5.00

Fig. 11. Periodical article request, illustrating change of title (ILL form)

Author (or periodical title, vol. and year)

I.R.E. Proceedings (N.Y., Institute of Radio Engineers, Inc.) [title changed to I.E.E.E. Proceedings] v.49, June 1961.

Title (with author & pages for periodical articles) (Incl. edition, place & date)   ☐ This edition only

"Frequency allocations for space communications." pages 1009-1015.

Verified in (or source of reference) and located through ULS 3:3013

article verified in Engr. I. 1961, p.1395.

If non-circulating, please supply ☐ Microfilm ☒ Hard copy if cost does not exceed $ 5.00

Fig. 12. Yearbooks, transactions, proceedings, etc. (ILL form)

NEWSPAPERS ON MICROFILM REQUESTS

Although lending of newspapers is ordinarily precluded by the difficulty and expense of shipping them, many libraries regularly lend newspapers on positive microfilm. Location of runs of newspapers may be determined through *Newspapers on Microfilm*. Generally, if you have a choice, request the newspaper from a library not located in the city where the newspaper was published; local newspapers are often in too heavy a demand in the home town to permit lending the film. Requests for loan of long runs of newspapers on microfilm should usually be limited to four reels at one time, the next group, if necessary, to be sent when those are returned.

Author (or periodical title, vol. and year)

Pall Mall Gazette. London. Jan. 1914–Nov. 1918.

Title (with author & pages for periodical articles) (Incl. edition, place & date)   ☐ This edition only

Verified in (or source of reference) NOM, 6th ed. p.424, states you have positive microfilm; may we borrow 4 reels at a time?

If non-circulating, please supply   ☐ Microfilm   ☐ Hard copy if cost does not exceed $_____

Fig. 13. Newspapers on microfilm (ILL form)

Newspapers should be entered under the name of the newspaper, followed by the place of publication (if place is not included in the title). Give full date wherever possible. If a specific article is wanted, particularly if the page is known, libraries with reader-printers can supply hard copy.

When requesting microforms, ascertain in advance whether the item is in microcard, microprint, microfiche, or microfilm and make sure the appropriate reading machine is available. When in doubt, indicate on the request what reading machines you have available.

REQUESTS IN NON-ROMAN ALPHABETS

Foreign-language materials, including serial titles, should always be requested in the original language (do not translate the title). Requests in non-Roman alphabets should be Romanized in form, accompanied by a slip giving the author and title in the original script, usually supplied by the reader (figure 14).

10. Request photocopy whenever practicable.

Read carefully chapter 5 on photocopy and copyright.

If the item wanted is relatively short (and does not contain illustrations that will not xerox satisfactorily) the borrowing librarian should order a photocopy, not request a loan. Not only periodical articles, but many pamphlets and some theses and dissertations are short enough to make photocopy, or at least micro- film, practical.

Interlibrary loan departments should consider having library funds budgeted for ordering photocopies of materials needed by their readers. Many libraries now follow this practice. Photoduplication orders can usually be handled more expeditiously if ordered on the ALA photoduplication order form (see appendix A).

REQUEST FOR BOOK	AUTHOR (PLEASE PRINT) :
	TITLE:
	PLACE: PUBLISHER: DATE:
REQUEST FOR PERIODICAL	NAME OF PERIODICAL: Kaizō 改造
	AUTHOR OF ARTICLE: Itō, Sei 伊藤 整
	TITLE OF ARTICLE: Seiji to bungei sakka 政治と文芸作家
	VOLUME No. v.33, no.14 PAGE Nos. 207-211 DATE OF VOL. 1952.
	PRINTED SOURCE OF REFERENCE: 雑誌記事索引・人文科学篇 v. 5, no. 10, p. 14.

Columbia University Libraries — INTERLIBRARY LOAN

For use of   Status   Dept.

Author (or periodical title, vol. and year)   SEE SLIP ATTACHED:
   Kaizō, v. 33, no. 14, 1952.

Title (with author & pages for periodical articles) (Incl. edition, place & date)   ☐ This edition only

   Itō, Sei, "Seiji to bungei sakka," p.207-211.

Verified in (or source of reference)   located in ULS 3:2260
      see also slip attached.
If noncirculating, please supply ☐ Microfilm   ☒ Hard copy if cost does not exceed $ 3.00

Fig. 14. Non-Roman-alphabet request with reader's manuscript slip (ILL form)

Borrowing libraries should indicate on the interlibrary loan form their willingness to accept and pay for photocopy. Consult Cosby Brinkley's *Directory of Institutional Photocopying Services* for listings of photographic services available and prices. Since it is almost as expensive to the lending library to make an estimate of photocopy charges as it is to make the photocopy, libraries should avoid requesting photocopy estimates unless the item is long or requires special handling.

If non-circulating, please supply ☐ Microfilm ☐ Hard copy if cost does not exceed $_____

Fig. 15. Photoduplication alternative (ILL form)

11. Revise all requests carefully before they are sent out. Sign requests.

Check all items on the request form, especially the citation, preferably against the original source in which the citation was verified. This step is particularly important for foreign-language materials. Typing should be neat, with no strikeovers. Accent marks, especially umlaut, should be clearly inserted in all copies of the request.

Detach and retain the D form. <u>Do not separate the A, B, and C forms.</u> Send the A, B, and C forms in a standard business window envelope, together with a three-by-five-inch self-addressed, gummed parcel return label (appendix B). Retain the D form as your interim record of the request (and to notify the lending library when the item is returned). Some libraries may wish to clip the reader's request workslip (see appendix C) to the D form for future reference. If there are carbons in your forms, do not remove the carbons, and do not detach from the stub.

Although the "National Interlibrary Loan Code, 1968" (section VI.2) recommends that in the interest of efficiency the lending library absorb costs which are nominal, such as for postage, some libraries that borrow more than they lend may want to help reduce the financial imbalance somewhat by continuing to reimburse postage and by sending a stamped return envelope with the initial request for the lending library's reply.

The librarian approving the loan request should sign (not initial) the request form.

Note: The receiving library assumes responsibility for notification of non-receipt.

AUTHORIZED BY: *Mary D Jones*
(FULL NAME) Title Mary D. Jones, Librarian

Fig. 16. Authorization signature (ILL form)

12. Follow all instructions and regulations of the lending library.

The lending library will send the B and C forms back to you indicating whether or not the item is being sent. The B form becomes the borrowing library's permanent record of the transaction. If the item is being sent, the lending library will probably enclose a return parcel post label (see appendix B). Use it; clip it to the D form so that it will be at hand when needed to send the book back; failure to use the return label may result in the item being reshelved in the lending library before the record of your having returned it has been discharged. The borrowing librarian should note on the B, C, and D forms the date the item was received, and the postage due, if any.

Any restrictions, such as "For use in library only" and "Copying not permitted" must, of course, be strictly observed. To protect manuscripts under

B INTERLIBRARY LOAN REQUEST
According to the A.L.A. Interlibrary Loan Code

REPORT REPORTS: Checked by J Smithson

SENT BY: [ ]   Library rate [✓]

Charges $ none   Insured for $ 50⁰⁰

Date sent Nov 5, 1969

DUE   Keep 4 weeks

RESTRICTIONS: [✓] For use in library only

[✓] Copying not permitted   [✓] Please have

Prof. Smith sign use slip
pasted in front of volume 1.

NOT SENT BECAUSE: [ ] In use

[ ] Non circulating   [ ] Not owned

Estimated Cost of: Microfilm_____

Hard copy_____

BORROWING LIBRARY RECORD:

Date received Nov. 13, 1969

Date returned Dec. 11, 1969

By [ ]   Library rate [✓]

Postage
enclosed $_____   Insured for $ 50.00

RENEWALS: *(Request and report on sheet C)*

Requested on Sorry, we do not

Renewed to   renew
(or period of renewal)

Fig. 17. Interlibrary loan form B report—borrowing library record

common-law copyright, some universities that lend theses and dissertations require the user to sign a statement of use of the manuscript. The borrowing librarian is responsible for seeing that this is done. If the item is not used by the reader, the borrowing librarian should enclose a note when returning the volume explaining why no signature was added to the list. The names of all readers who wish to use a dissertation should be included in the original request; some major libraries lend for the exclusive use of the individual whose name appears on the request. All users must sign the statement.

13. Return materials promptly. Pack them well. Send notice of return separately.

The borrowing library must, of course, return the item within the time limits set by the lending library. Renewals should be requested only in emergencies; if it is necessary to request a renewal, the request should be sent in time to reach the lending library before the date the material was due. Send the renewal request on the C form, Interim Report.

Pack the item well, protecting especially the corners of the volume. Jiffy bags, if used, should be new and the correct size to protect the volume. Journals, theses, and other large, heavy volumes need more protection than jiffy bags give. The Library Technology Program has developed a reusable carton for interlibrary loan shipments. Other commercially produced shipping containers are available. If the lending library sends you the item in such a carton, be sure to save the carton and return the volume in it.

If the item is sent to you in a carton containing library markings, such as microfilm boxes or slipcases, be sure that this carton is returned to the lending library. Loss of this box may mean that a new box must be relabeled before the item can be returned to the shelf.

Special care should be taken to prevent pamphlets from being lost in transit, when unpacking shipments, and while the pamphlet is being used in the borrowing library. Since pamphlets often have soft covers, stiff boards should be used by both the lending and the borrowing library to prevent bending of the covers during mailing.

Affix the lending library's return-address label; add the name and address of the borrowing library. All correspondence and shipments should be conspicuously labelled "Interlibrary Loan." Manuscript material should always be insured; the lending library's instructions regarding insurance of other shipments should be followed.

Insert the C form in the book during its return shipment, to assist in identifying the transaction both in your own shipping room and in the lending library.

The D form, Notice of Return, together with stamps to cover postal reimbursement to those few institutions that still require reimbursement, should be sent *separately,* not in the parcel with the item, at the time the loan is returned.

SUMMARY CHECKLIST

1. Follow the Interlibrary Loan Code.
2. Instruct your readers.
3. Screen requests carefully.
4. Verify citations.
5. Provide accurate and complete bibliographic citations.
6. Do not use initials or abbreviations unless they are part of the actual title of the item.
7. Find out before sending the request what library owns the item wanted.
8. Check the lending policy of the lending library.
9. Follow the directions on the interlibrary loan forms carefully and supply all relevant information.
10. Request photocopy when practicable.
11. Revise requests carefully.
12. Follow all instructions and regulations of the lending library.
13. Return materials properly.

4/Instructions for Lending Libraries

SUPPLIES

Minimum supplies needed:

    3x5 self-addressed, gummed return shipping labels (see appendix B)

    Adequate packing supplies

Additional supplies recommended:

    Your institution's photocopy price lists for distribution to borrowing libraries

    3x5 gummed shipping labels with address section blank, your address as sender (see appendix B)

    Standard window envelopes

    Form letters indicating your lending policies

    Form letters indicating inadequacies in the requests (see appendix E)

    Extra copies of reprints of the "National Interlibrary Loan Code" and of your own local or regional code

    Rubber stamps for most commonly needed instructions, such as "Please give verification or source of reference on all requests" and "Please give author, title, and page for periodical articles."

INSTRUCTIONS

1. Publicize your interlibrary loan and photocopy policies and regulations.

Have a copy of your regulations available to send to the libraries that regularly borrow from you. State and regional associations that compile and ratify local codes should publish a supplementary interlibrary loan manual giving interlibrary loan and photocopy policies of the region's resource libraries. Cooperate in this project.

All libraries may find that form letters clarifying policies and explaining actions taken help to promote better understanding and cooperation and result in fewer inadequate requests. (See appendixes D–K.)

Limit your interlibrary loan policy statement to important items, as clear and simple as possible, following national and local codes. Information should include usually:

> Full address to which interlibrary loan requests should be sent
>
> Departments (if any) that do their own lending, to which requests should be sent directly, with addresses
>
> TWX number and policy regarding teletypewriter requests
>
> Types of libraries or readers for which the lending library will not ordinarily give service
>
> Automatic photocopy substitution policy
>
> Lending policy for serials, microforms, theses, and dissertations (other forms if restricted)
>
> Major noncirculating collections
>
> Photocopy fees and services available
>
> (Other fees)

2. Have adequate, well-trained and well-supervised staff.

Have enough staff to devote adequate attention to the volume of interlibrary loan requests that you receive. Carefully train and supervise nonprofessional assistants. Emphasize the importance of prompt action on requests and meticulous record keeping. Have the shipping room staff regularly warned about adequate packing, correct labels on the packages, adequate insurance, etc.

As states work toward the development of networks and reimbursement of lending costs, the increase in overall efficiency of interlibrary loan procedures, the maintenance of accurate statistics, and the gathering of accurate and comprehensive data on costs of interlibrary loan transactions become increasingly important. Statistics on number of interlibrary loan transactions involving items borrowed and items lent, with a subdivision on returnable and nonreturnable items lent, are collected at intervals by the United States Office of Education, Library Surveys Branch. In addition, libraries should keep statistics on the number of requests to borrow they make that are not filled, and the number of requests addressed to them that they are unable to lend.

3. Process requests as soon as possible.

One of the major dissatisfactions with conventional interlibrary loan is the length of time the request sometimes stays in the lending library while being processed, especially if the lending library is large and has to send to one of its departmental libraries for the item. Establish a regular routine to ensure that incoming requests, especially requests for items that must be obtained from departmental libraries, receive systematic review and follow-up.

Try to send the requested material and report as promptly as possible. Each library must decide its own policy regarding priorities in filling requests. While it may be desirable that all interlibrary loan requests be sent within twenty-four hours, this is frequently impossible.

Specific agreements are sometimes made between reciprocating libraries to give priority to each other's teletype requests. Other libraries feel that interlibrary loan requests should be filled in order of receipt, unless a deadline need is explained in the request.

4. Search card catalog carefully.

Read the request form carefully to determine the actual entry. Try a variety of approaches; entries vary from library to library. Have an experienced professional librarian recheck items not found. Take special care when checking entries reported in union catalogs and union lists to be owned by your library, and include a note of explanation on the requests for any items not found.

5. Verify requests not found in the card catalog as cited.

Admittedly this recommendation is controversial and involves policy decisions that are wholly within the province of the individual library and its interlibrary loan personnel. Indeed, the "National Interlibrary Loan Code, 1968" and the model state code both state that, if the request does not indicate a verification or original source of reference and the bibliographic data appear to be incorrect, the request may be returned unfilled without special effort to identify the reference.

Some libraries feel that the burden of verification should be placed on the borrowing library, which has access to the reader. Many libraries refuse to do searching for repeated offenders, especially if they do not even fill out the interlibrary loan request form properly. A form letter or note should be sent to the borrowing library pointing out the lack of adequate citation and verification. (See appendix E.)

Verification by lending libraries considerably increases the proportion of interlibrary loan requests filled.[1] Some libraries use the verification of unlocated interlibrary loan requests as an invaluable training device for new staff members, to acquaint them with the peculiarities of their own card catalog, available bibliographic resources, methodology, and the importance of exact citation in all reference work.

Most resource libraries are much more willing to help verify citations if there is clear indication on the request form that the borrowing library had exhausted its own resources.

Many state libraries are developing referral plans for contracting verification and location assistance, with remuneration to the resource libraries or regional catalogs for this service.

---

[1]Thomson, "General Interlibrary Loan Services," p.125–28, 162.

6. Educate the borrowing libraries.

The "National Interlibrary Loan Code, 1968" states that lending libraries have the responsibility of informing any borrowing library of its apparent failure to follow the provisions of the code. For this purpose, some lending libraries have reprints of the code available to send to libraries that ignore the code's provisions, and mark the relevant sections. Form letters may also be helpful (see appendix E).

It is especially important to encourage libraries that request materials you do not have, to attempt to ascertain locations before sending requests, especially if your library's holdings are reported regularly to the National Union Catalog and appear in *New Serial Titles* and the *Union List of Serials*. Suggest to borrowing libraries that ask for inexpensive in-print material that they purchase the material rather than request a loan.

Nevertheless, in the interests of cooperation and good will, if the first request you receive from a library is inadequate, try to make an exception to your usual requirements and fill the request, pointing out the inadequacies.

7. If the item is not owned or is noncirculating, supply additional information, if available.

Suggest locations, if the information is readily available. Correct any inaccuracies in the citation, in order that the borrowing library can send correctly to another library. Give pagination for noncirculating periodical articles, in order that the borrowing library can readily order a photocopy. It is extremely helpful to small libraries that do not have *Dissertation Abstracts,* if you will send them the order number and price of noncirculating dissertations available from University Microfilms. (See appendix D.)

8. Give prompt, clear reports on requests.

Be as explicit as possible in replying to requests. Indicate clearly on the request whether you are sending the item, sending a photocopy, or not sending the item. Answer any questions on use of the materials asked by the borrowing library, to save further correspondence.

Mark the request "not owned" only if the library has none of the item requested; if the lending library has part of the set, but not the item wanted, indicate "Vols. 210-217 lacking" or "have parts 1 and 9 only." For dissertations and theses, it is helpful if you indicate "dissertation not yet deposited" or "no record of any student by this name."

Unless the borrowing library has checked "This edition only," send the latest edition available, but explain the discrepancy on the request form; for example, "sending 3d ed. 4th not owned," or "sending 4th ed., later eds. in use or on reserve."

If the item is not available because it is in use or at the bindery, suggest when to re-request, or state clearly that a hold has been placed. Libraries should keep a regular check on all holds placed.

If you are lending the item, write the call number on the A, B, and C forms, together with the date sent, the date due, and the amount of insurance. As explained in the code, "unless otherwise specified by the lending library, the duration of loan is normally calculated to mean the period of time the item may remain with the borrowing library, disregarding the time spent in transit." However, if you want an item returned by a precise date, you should so indicate; for example, "Due back at NjParB by March 1." Some libraries have found that a four-week loan period with no renewals works well for them. Be as generous in setting the loan period as the needs of your own readers for the particular item permit.

Supply a clear statement on any restrictions on use. If you require that material you send on interlibrary loan be used in the borrowing library only, state this on the request. If you wish to restrict photocopy, check "Copying not permitted." If you require a signature of use for a dissertation or thesis, this should be indicated. Note any extraordinary condition of the item on the request.

Retain form A for your records. Send forms B and C to the borrowing library. If there is a delay in the shipment, notify the borrowing library by returning form C, appropriately annotated. If the item is being shipped, form B should be mailed to the borrowing library separately from the item. Inserting form C in the volume during shipping helps identify the transaction both in your own shipping room, and in the borrowing library. Writing the name of the borrowing library on the date due slip may also reduce the probability of misrouting of materials. Include a mailing label addressed to the lending library to ensure correct return. (See appendix B.)

9. Consider all reasonable requests for exceptions to policy.

While flexible regulations are sometimes difficult to administer, try to make exceptions if the readers in your own library will not be inconvenienced.

10. Search for missing items.

Misshelving of materials and inadequate circulation records, especially for materials used in the library building, in carrels, or in faculty offices, may sometimes be the cause of interlibrary loan failures. Search carefully for missing items.

11. Pack and ship carefully.

Pack adequately, especially large heavy volumes, and pamphlets and small items. Protect corners with cardboards. Be sure the right parcel label is affixed to the right parcel; mix-ups are common. (See also page 41.)

Insure adequately. It is especially important to insure theses and dissertations and other unique material. Some libraries that do a large volume of lending find it economical to contract with companies for blanket insurance, sometimes used on an insert coupon basis.

Comply with requests for airmail and special-delivery service. The borrowing library should, of course, reimburse you for this.

Shipment will usually be made by parcel post, library materials rate. The "National Interlibrary Loan Code, 1968" recommends that in the interest of efficiency, the lending library absorb nominal costs, as for postage. Use the B form to notify the borrowing library of shipment, and send this form separately from the material itself.

12. Be able to supply photocopy.

Have a simple provision for payment of photocopies, an arrangement for deposit accounts, or provision for cumulative billing. Make reciprocal credit transfer arrangements with libraries near you. Send photocopies by first-class mail unless very bulky.

13. Participate in interlibrary cooperative activities.

Participate in state and regional cooperative service organizations, regional lists and catalogs, directories, interlibrary loan workshops, and liberalized regional lending agreements. Efficient regional sharing of resources speeds accessibility, particularly where truck routing and rapid communication systems can be developed, and spreads the interlibrary lending responsibility more evenly among participating libraries.

SUMMARY CHECKLIST

1. Publicize your interlibrary loan and photocopy policies and regulations.
2. Have adequate, well-trained, and well-supervised staff.
3. Process requests as soon as possible.
4. Search card catalog carefully.
5. Verify requests not found in the card catalog as cited.
6. Educate the borrowing libraries.
7. If the item is not owned or is noncirculating, supply additional information, if available.
8. Give prompt, clear reports on requests.
9. Consider all reasonable requests for exceptions to policy.
10. Search for missing items.
11. Pack and ship carefully.
12. Be able to supply photocopy.
13. Participate in interlibrary cooperative activities.

5/Photocopy, Copyright, and Reprinting

SUMMARY OF ILL CODE PROVISIONS REGARDING PHOTOCOPY AND COPYRIGHT

The provisions of the "National Interlibrary Loan Code, 1968" (see chapter 1) regarding photocopy and copyright are:

Sec. V.1.   Any type of library material needed for the purpose of research may be requested on loan or in photocopy from another library. The lending library has the privilege of deciding in each case whether a particular item should or should not be provided, and whether the original or a copy should be sent.

Sec. VI.1.   The borrowing library assumes the responsibility for all costs charged by the lending library, including transportation, insurance, copying, and any service charges. If the charges are more than nominal, and not authorized beforehand by the borrowing library, the lending library should inform the requesting library and ask for authorization to proceed with the transaction. Borrowing libraries should try to anticipate charges, such as for copies, and authorize them on the original request.

Sec. VII.3.   Unless specifically forbidden by the lending library, copying by the borrowing library is permitted provided that it is in accordance with copyright law and American Library Association policy.

Sec. IX.4.   A standard ALA interlibrary loan form should be used for each item requested (or an ALA photoduplication order form, when it is known that copies will be supplied and payment required).

COPYRIGHT LAW AND ALA POLICY

Interpretation of copyright law is in continuous process of revision, particularly in the light of congressional hearings on pending legislation and of court decisions. Each library should determine its own policy in the context of current law and precedent, including the concept of "fair use."[1] An excellent sum-

---

[1] The ALA Joint Committee on Fair Use in Photocopying issued a statement in the *Library Journal* 90:3403–3405 (Sept. 1, 1965).

mary by Charles F. Gosnell of the problems of copyright and reproduction by libraries appears as an appendix in William R. Hawken's *Copying Methods Manual.*[2]

LIBRARY PHOTODUPLICATION SERVICE

The almost universal practice among libraries of providing a photocopy substitute for parts of volumes, particularly serials, has several advantages but it also presents a number of administrative problems. The advantages are obvious: the lending library is able to retain the original so that it is available for the use of its own clientele (and it is not subject to loss or damage in the mails), while the borrower obtains a copy which he may keep permanently in his files. The disadvantages—problems of varying charges, of billing and payment, and of differences in substitution practices—are equally obvious. It has not yet been possible to get libraries to agree on uniform rates or policies, partly because of differences in the administration of photocopying services staffing and of the varying requirements of institutional business offices. Problems are also caused by the refusal of some libraries to circulate any serial publication, regardless of the infrequency of its use or the length of the material needed.

The following suggestions for minimizing present difficulties are offered.

1. Obtain the latest edition of Cosby Brinkley's *Directory of Institutional Photocopying Services* and refer to it for information on rates, addresses, etc.

2. Provide in the library budget for the cost of photocopy substitutions and do not ask for reimbursement from patrons. (This will eliminate the pressures to search for circulating copies and the cheapest services and the temptation to evade the rule in the code about placement of requests.)

3. To avoid delay in service, authorize photocopy substitution on the original request.

4. Where it is possible, establish deposit accounts with photoduplication services (the Library of Congress and the New York Public Library provide such accounts).

---

[2]Charles F. Gosnell, "Appendix C Copyright," in William R. Hawken *Copying Methods Manual,* LTP Publication no.10 (Chicago: Library Technology Program, American Library Assn., 1966), p.309–16.

See also: "[ALA] Council Takes Stand on Copyright Legislation," *ALA Bulletin* 62:275–77 (March 1968); " 'Fair Use' under Copyright Faces Court Test," *ALA Bulletin* 62:616 (June 1968); Edward G. Freehafer, "Summary Statement of Policy of the Joint Libraries Committee on Fair Use in Photocopying," *Special Libraries* 55:104–106 (Feb. 1964); Verner Clapp, *Copyright: A Librarian's View* (Washington, D.C.: Assn. of Research Libraries, 1968); idem, "Copyright Dilemma: A Librarian's View," *Library Quarterly* 38:352–87 (Oct. 1968).

5. If a deposit account cannot be established, ask a regularly supplying library if bills can be cumulated and sent on a quarterly or semiannual basis.

6. Libraries having a relatively balanced exchange of photocopies may agree to supply each other free of charge.

PHOTOCOPY ACQUISITION

Libraries should not ordinarily borrow volumes for the sole purpose of making a copy. Material to be added to a library's collection—e.g., xerox of missing pages or a microfilm of a book—should be ordered from the owning library through the regular acquisitions procedure, using the ALA photoduplication order form (see appendix A). If the owning library does not have copying facilities, it may lend the volume.

LENDING FOR REPRINTING

Publishers desiring copies of books for reprinting should not make requests on interlibrary loan, since such transactions do not come within the definition of interlibrary loan. Any person or organization borrowing a publication must not use it for reprinting purposes without the specific permission in writing of the lending library. The Reprinting Committee, Acquisitions Section, Resources and Technical Services Division of ALA has published a general policy on reprinting from library materials.[3] (A sample policy statement is given in appendix K.)

---

[3]"Lending to Reprinters: Policy Statement of the Reprinting Committee," *Library Resources and Technical Services* 12:455–56 (Fall 1968) and 14:138 (Winter 1970).

6/Requesting Locations from the Union Catalog Division of the Library of Congress

HOW TO REQUEST LOCATIONS

The Union Catalog Division of the Library of Congress will, within the limits described below, attempt to respond to requests from libraries and individuals for location of materials in a majority of the large research libraries of the United States. A detailed description of the National Union Catalog will be found on pages 98–100. There is no membership involved in the use of the National Union Catalog.

Local and nearby resources, and published bibliographies and union lists, should be exhausted before a search of the National Union Catalog is requested. A critical space shortage and the requirements of the National Union Catalog Publication Project have led to a scattering and proliferation of the various segments of the National Union Catalog. The Union Catalog Division therefore has asked that libraries requesting locations of information use the form LC 69-42 (figure 18), with one title only listed on each form; this procedure facilitates separate searches or the special routing of many requests to other areas of the Library of Congress, and permits the staff to organize its work more efficiently. Location requests for 1956 and later titles, which are being cumulated for reporting in the 1962–67 quinquennial and the next issue of the *Register of Additional Locations,* are not accessible for checking. Cards being edited for the *National Union Catalog, Pre-1956 Imprints* are also not available.

Requesting libraries are asked to use special care in verifying the name of the author, title, and imprint, following the procedure described on pages 20–23. Furnish as complete a citation as possible, following examples on pages 28–38. State source of verification, or, if item cannot be verified, give the original source with citation in full form. If a particular edition is not required, please state "any edition." If not all volumes of a multivolume set (monograph or series) are required, designate the specific volume or volumes required.

Prepare request forms in triplicate, submitting *two* to the Union Catalog Division, Library of Congress, Washington, D.C. 20540, and keeping the other

Request for Locations of Title
(Submit in Duplicate)

For LC Use Only

Searched In:

(This title has been verified in sources as indicated.)

From

⌐ Interlibrary Loan Librarian
Bergen Community College
400 Paramus Road
Paramus, New Jersey
　　　　　Zip Code: 07652 ⌐

☐ NUC　　　☐ NUC, 19

☐ NUC Suppl.　☐

☐ Main Catalog　☐

☐ ULS　　　☐ BM

☐ NST　　　☐ BN

Author
Bible. O. T. Psalms. Latin, 1884.

Fold—

Title
The Psalter of Psalms of David and
certain canticles, with a translation and
exposition in English by Richard Rolle of
Hampole; ed. from manuscripts by the Rev.
H. R. Bramley. . .Oxford, Clarendon Press,
1884

Report:

☐ Not Located

Located:

Verified in　　LC Cat – 1942　　14:125

To

⌐ 　　　　　　　　　　　　　　　　⌐

Union Catalog Division
Library of Congress
Washington, D.C. 20540

LC 69-42 (12/67)

Fig. 18. Request for locations of title form to the Union Catalog Division

for your records. The Union Catalog Division will mark locations on one of the copies and return it to you, as expeditiously as possible.

It is hoped that printed forms will be commercially available in the near future (as of January, 1970). In the meantime, libraries may wish to reproduce their own copies on 5¼-by-8-inch paper. Libraries that do not have these forms may send a limited number of requests to the Union Catalog Division on standard interlibrary loan request forms. Leave the *lending library space blank* so that location symbols may be written in this space. Indicate at the top of the form "Request for location only" and address the envelope to the Union Catalog Division.

Procedure for requesting locations by teletypewriter are described on pages 58–62.

Because of the pressure of regular duties, the Union Catalog Division staff cannot undertake to search long lists, but competent persons can be suggested who will do the work for a reasonable remuneration.

NUC SYMBOLS AND HOW TO REQUEST ONE

The symbols used in the National Union Catalog are unique for each library. For libraries in the United States the letters indicate: first, the state in which the library is located; second (usually but not invariably), the city; and third, the name of the library. These symbols are useful in a variety of ways, whether or not the library sends cards of its holdings to the National Union Catalog. If local and regional union lists use these symbols, the lists and catalogs so compiled can be merged or regrouped and incorporated into other lists without reediting. Listings of the symbols are regularly published.[1] For teletype answer-back codes, use of the NUC symbol plus the name of the city results in a unique symbol readily understood by all, and prevents the confusion that may result if several libraries arbitrarily select the same symbol for themselves. If you do not know the NUC symbol for your library, or if you think it does not have one, and you would like to request one, simply write to the Union Catalog Division, Library of Congress, Washington, D.C. 20540, and you will be notified of the symbol that has been assigned to your library.

---

[1]*Symbols of American Libraries* (10th ed., 1969, of *Symbols Used in the National Union Catalog of the Library of Congress*) is available from the Card Division, Library of Congress, Building 159, Navy Yard Annex, Washington, D.C. 20541, price $1.

7/Teletypewriter Requests

GENERAL INSTRUCTIONS

Libraries using teletypewriter communication for interlibrary loan and photo-duplication requests are urged to become familiar with the policies, standards, procedures, and instructions described in detail in Warren Bird's *Teletypewriter Exchange System for Interlibrary Communication* (Durham, N.C.: Duke University Medical Center Library, January 1968).[1]

The format to be used for teletypewriter requests (described below, and illustrated in figures 19–23) is based on the standard ALA interlibrary loan request form. This spacing and arrangement permits easy interfiling and processing, and folding and mailing in window envelopes when necessary. All information required in the interlibrary loan form should be included except the address of the lending library. Two-copy paper (with one interleaving carbon) is used at both the sending and receiving stations, providing four total copies for filing, permanent record, and mailing when required. (See appendix L.) Interlibrary loan requests should be separated by ten to twelve line feeds to ensure room for making up ALA interlibrary loan form size copy.

Lending libraries may find it useful to have a rubber stamp made duplicating the report stub of the Interlibrary Loan Request form (the right side, see figure 17.) This stamped information can be used to check the appropriate reply and the resulting form sent to the borrowing library as their copy, report B.

Libraries considering the installation of a teletypewriter should plan carefully for a location which is readily accessible, but where the noise of the machine will not distract staff or readers. Acoustically treated cases for teletypewriters may be purchased or constructed locally.

Desired equipment capabilities are listed in appendix 2 of *Teletypewriter Exchange System for Interlibrary Communication*.

Tape transmission is much more accurate, faster, and less expensive than direct transmission. Unless specific agreements to the contrary are made, the

---

[1]Available on request. Available for $2 from the same source is *Library Telecommunications Directory: Canada–United States* (1969), compiled by Warren Bird and David Skene Melvin.

borrowing library pays all teletypewriter message fees, both sending and receiving.[2]

MESSAGE FORMAT

1. Lending library identification code.

The answer-back code for the lending library must begin every message, so that messages may be identified when removed from the machine. Libraries are urged to use as their answer-back code the National Union Catalog location symbol, followed by the name of the city. The NUC symbol is unique and its use will avoid the confusion of several libraries selecting the same symbol. Libraries that do not have a symbol assigned by the Library of Congress Union Catalog Division should request one; the procedure is explained on pages 53–54.

Send one extra line feed.

2. Message type, serial number, and date.

Standard abbreviations identify the type of message:

UC   —National Union Catalog Requests
ILLRQ—Interlibrary Loan Requests
ILLRP—Interlibrary Loan Report and Renewal Response
ILLRN—Interlibrary Loan Renewal Request

The type of message code is followed by the serial number of the message (each message sent should be numbered sequentially) and the date. Message date should be in standard telecommunication format, e.g., 22/JAN/70 (day/ month/year). This provides unique identification for each message when replying. When several requests are included in a single message transmission, each and every separate request must bear its own lending library code, date, identification number, and return address, since each transaction may be cut apart from the others and handled and shipped separately.

Send three extra line feeds.

3. Borrowing library's full name and address.

Many lending libraries will use this portion of the message as their shipping label, and it should be spaced and written out in full, including ZIP code.

Send three extra line feeds.

---

[2]It is suggested that staff time and tolls can be substantially reduced by reciprocal agreements between libraries which frequently call each other to send reports by direct paid call. It is possible to make credit transfer arrangements similar to those made for reciprocal balancing of photoduplication costs.

4. Reader's name, status, and department.

Send one extra line feed.

5. Bibliographic citation to desired item.

Citation should be given in full, not abbreviated, and should follow format outlined on pages 22–23 and 28–38.

6. Verification. See pages 20–22 and 24.

7. Authorizing librarian.

Send three extra line feeds.

8. Remarks.

Send three extra line feeds.

9. Message ending.

At its completion, each message must end with the word *end* and the type and serial number of that message, followed by the identification code (answer-back code) of the borrowing library. Some regional networks find that it is helpful if the last message of each batch is followed by a slash followed by the initials of the sender.

Ten to twelve line feeds should separate each message.

RENEWAL REQUESTS

Teletypewriter requests for renewals of loans must list author, title, edition, imprint, and the call number, if known. Include the message number of the original request. Approval will be assumed unless denial of renewal is made by collect teletypewriter call.

Unless specific agreements exist to the contrary, do not expect that the lending library will be able to identify your renewal request merely by the message number of the original request.

REPORTS AND RENEWAL REPLIES

Replies to interlibrary loan requests and renewal replies should be transmitted by teletypewriter within twenty-four hours whenever possible. Teletypewriter reports should be made if material cannot be sent or if there is to be a delay. Reports are not required if materials or photocopies are being sent. If original

```
 DNLMBETHESDA

 ILLRQ 88 19/APR/66



 INTERLIBRARY LOAN
 DUKE UNIVERSITY MEDICAL CENTER LIBRARY
 DURHAM, NORTH CAROLINA 27706



 DR. SAMUEL M. ATKINSON RESIDENT OB-GYN

 NEW ZEALAND MEDICAL JOURNAL  V. 59 (DEC) 1960
 LILEY, A.W.  : TECHNIQUES AND COMPLICATION OF AMNIOCENTESIS
   581-596
 VER:  CIM 2: A-844, 1961
 AUTHR:  J. BROWN



 REMARKS: VOLUME NOT IN AREA



 END  ILLRQ 88
 NCD-M DURHAM
 END
```

Fig. 19. Periodical article request by teletype

materials are being sent, form B (the carbon copy) should be marked with date due and restrictions, if any, and mailed to the borrowing library.

Include in the teletypewriter report the borrowing library's code, serial number of request, and the date of the original request. Use phrases such as those listed on the Not Sent Because section of the ALA Interlibrary Loan Request form.

NATIONAL UNION CATALOG REQUESTS

An increase in the number of requests for location received by teletype has coincided with the growth and scattering of the files that must be searched by the Union Catalog Division. Teletype messages, especially the longer ones, create problems in the search for locations. Special forms and clerical procedures involved in returning messages by teletypewriter also contribute to a decision to adopt a policy of returning some of the TWX messages by regular mail. The Union Catalog Division will continue to accept inquiries in teletype form, but a

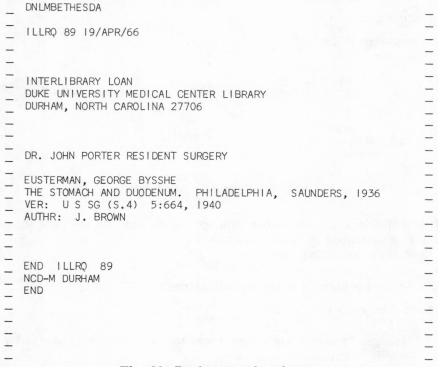

```
    DNLMBETHESDA

    ILLRQ 89 19/APR/66



    INTERLIBRARY LOAN
    DUKE UNIVERSITY MEDICAL CENTER LIBRARY
    DURHAM, NORTH CAROLINA 27706



    DR. JOHN PORTER RESIDENT SURGERY

    EUSTERMAN, GEORGE BYSSHE
    THE STOMACH AND DUODENUM.  PHILADELPHIA,  SAUNDERS, 1936
    VER:  U S SG (S.4) 5:664, 1940
    AUTHR:  J. BROWN



    END  ILLRQ  89
    NCD-M DURHAM
    END
```

Fig. 20. Book request by teletype

portion of the replies will be returned through the mails. Relative distance, the likelihood of delay in transmission because of weekends and holidays, and workload will be the determining factors.

MESSAGE FORMAT FOR NUC REQUESTS

Limit the length of the lines of text to six inches and leave right and left margins of at least an inch. Allow for three horizontal spaces between entries. This spacing is needed to permit notation of the results of search.

1. Message: "LIB CONG US UNION CATALOG DIVISION"

Name the division of the Library of Congress to which the message is to be delivered. Requests concerning book locations should be sent to the Union Catalog Division; those pertaining only to interlibrary loan transactions should be addressed to the Loan Division. Messages are not received directly in either

```
 _   NCU-H CHAPEL HILL                                              _
 _                                                                  _
 _   ILLRP 71   11/APR/66                                           _
 _                                                                  _
 _                                                                  _
 _   YOUR ILLRQ 43 10/APR/66 NOT SENT BECAUSE: THIS ISSUE NOT OWNED  _
 _                                                                  _
 _                                                                  _
 _   END ILLRP  71                                                  _
 _   NCD-M DURHAM                                                   _
 _   END
```

Fig. 21. Teletype report format

of these divisions and designation of a specific division will eliminate the possibility of misrouting by the receiving unit.

Send three extra line feeds.

2. Borrowing library's full name and address.

Send three extra line feeds.

3. Message: "REQUEST LOCATIONS FROM NUC PLS ANS TWX COL (and your number)"

Send three extra line feeds.

4. Message type (UC), serial number, and date.

5. Citation and verification.

Requests should be organized and listed separately in the following categories:

    a. Western-language monographs: imprints before 1956
    b. Western-language monographs: imprints after 1955
    c. Serials
    d. Orientalia (Hebrew, Chinese, Japanese, etc.)
    e. Slavic materials printed in the Cyrillic alphabet.

Separate listings are requested because the searching must be done in dispersed and separate files; use of separate lists permits more expeditious routing and searching of items falling in different categories. Each portion of the list may then be returned as its search is completed instead of being held until all items have been searched. Breaking the list down into categories also helps to reduce the number of cumbersomely long lists.

Send three extra line feeds.

LIB CONG US UNION CATALOG DIVISION

REFERENCE DIVISION
DUKE UNIVERSITY MEDICAL CENTER LIBRARY
DURHAM, NORTH CAROLINA 27706

REQUEST LOCATIONS FROM NUC PLS
ANS TWX COL 510 927 1816

UC 17 12/JAN/69
LAMBE, WILLIAM
RESEARCHES INTO THE PROPERTIES OF SPRING WATER.
LONDON, J. JOHNSON, 1803
VER: LC CAT -1942 83:558

REFERENCE DIVISION
DUKE UNIVERSITY MEDICAL CENTER LIBRARY
DURHAM, NORTH CAROLINA 27706
510 827 1816

UC 18 12/JAN/69
CALVET PRATS, FERNANDO
BIOQUIMICA PARA MEDICOS, QUIMECOS, Y FARMACEUTICOS
MADRID, EDITORIAL ALHAMBRA, 1956
VER: NUC 1953-57, 4:410
REMARKS: DNLM COPY MISSING

M. A. BROWN, REF LIBN
END UC 17, 18, 12/JAN/69
NCD-M DURHAM

Fig. 22. Search request by teletype to the National Union Catalog

```
—  NCD-M DURHAM                                               —
—  710 822 0185 CLG COL OK TO ACCEPT GA PLS        OK GAP     —
                                                             —
—  UC 17 12/JAN/69 LAMBE, MH, DNLM, PPPH, PU, PPCP, NNNAM    —
—  UC 18 10/JAN/69 CALVET, DNLM ONLY                         —
                                                             —
—  END OF MSG PLS ACK                                        —
—  OK TNX END                                                —
—                                                            —
—                                                            —
—                                                            —
—                                                            —
```

Fig. 23. Reply by teletype to National Union Catalog request

6. Second message type, etc., bibliographic citation, and verification in same category.

List the items to be searched in each category in alphabetical order by author (or title if the author is not known or the work is anonymous) and, in the case of more than one work by the same author, subarrange alphabetically by title.

7. Next category of materials.

Repeat the *name, address, and teletype number* of the inquiring library at the head of each category of titles and leave an open space of six lines between the separate categories. With this spacing and identification, the list can be cut into segments that can be searched and returned separately.

Send three extra line feeds.

8. Authorizing librarian.

9. Message ending.

8/Dissertations and Theses on Microfilm

GENERAL INSTRUCTIONS

Obtaining theses and dissertations on interlibrary loan is not simple.[1] The 1968 "National Interlibrary Loan Code" includes "typescript doctoral dissertations, when fully reproduced in microfilm and readily available" among the classes of materials that libraries should not ordinarily ask to borrow, since they are considered to fall within the class of inexpensive United States materials in print.

Some universities do not have their dissertations microfilmed commercially, and microfilms must be ordered through the photoduplication service of the university. Cosby Brinkley's *Directory of Institutional Photocopying Services* indicates for each university:

> Dissertations accepted between _____ (date) and _____ (date) are available for loan.
>
> Dissertations accepted by our university since _____ (date) have been microfilmed by:
>
> _____University Microfilms
>
> _____Ourselves

ORDERING FROM UNIVERSITY MICROFILMS

Dissertation Abstracts is a monthly compilation of abstracts of doctoral dissertations submitted for filming to University Microfilms, Inc. (UM) by more than 250 cooperating institutions. Some institutions do not send all of their doctoral dissertations. Also, institutions began using UM at different times. Recent issues of *Dissertation Abstracts* list Cooperating Institutions for the Doctoral Dissertation Series, including the dates when institutions first began

---

[1]Jane W. Gatliff and S. Foreman, "Interlibrary Loan Policies on Dissertations and Serial Publications," *College and Research Libraries* 25:209–11 (May 1964); J. Plotkin, "Dissertations and Interlibrary Loan," *RQ* 4:5–9 (Jan. 1965).

to use UM services. These dates do not necessarily indicate the dates of the earliest dissertations filmed by UM for each institution. Some universities on entering the program decided to publish earlier dissertations through UM. Other schools used the program for publishing only those dissertations that were ready at the time of entry or later. University Microfilms does not require institutions that send their dissertations to UM for filming to agree to discontinue lending typescripts or microfilms of these dissertations. The decision is solely within the province of the individual library to continue to lend typescripts or microfilm copies, or not, as it wishes.

It is the policy of University Microfilms when filming a dissertation to reproduce on film all visual material submitted to it, including folded illustrations, large geology maps, engineering drawings, etc. Colors are reproduced in black and white. These materials are filmed in accordance with the latest USA Standards. Of necessity they usually have to be filmed on more than one frame, and sometimes the reduction ratio differs from that in the text. University Microfilms cannot, of course, photograph audiotapes, audiodiscs, and other nonvisual material.

Complete copies of dissertations listed in *Dissertation Abstracts* may be purchased from University Microfilms in either positive 35mm microfilm copies, or enlarged xerographic prints. The minimum charge is three dollars per dissertation, plus shipping and handling charges and any applicable taxes. Only complete dissertations, not selected pages, will be furnished. For certain types of illustrative materials, photographic (silver) enlargements are recommended.[2]

Prices for microfilm and bound xerographic copies appear at the end of each abstract in *Dissertation Abstracts*. Order by order number and name of author. The order number appears directly under the abstract title. Do not order by LC card number. Libraries that wish to order a dissertation and that do not have *Dissertation Abstracts* available for verification should arrange with a large library nearby to verify the author, title, order number, and price for them.

To expedite orders of dissertations:

1. Order by order number and author's name.
2. Do not send payment with your order; you will be invoiced at the time of shipment for material ordered and necessary handling and shipping charges.
3. Send your order to University Microfilms, 300 North Zeeb Road, Ann Arbor, Michigan 48106.

Postage-paid order cards, shown in figure 24, are available on request from University Microfilms.

---

[2]Prices, available upon request, are subject to change without notice.

University Microfilms is cooperating with a committee of the Association of Research Libraries in speeding up filming of dissertations and filling orders. However, variation in seasonal demand results in considerable variation in elapsed time in filling orders.

Please enter my order for the following dissertations:

❶
Order
Number

❷
Author's Last Name and Initials

❸
Please check *type* of copy you are ordering

35mm Positive Microfilm	Softbound xerographic copy	Clothbound xerographic copy*
[ ]	[ ]	[ ]
[ ]	[ ]	[ ]
[ ]	[ ]	[ ]
[ ]	[ ]	[ ]

❹ Bill to:

❺ Ship to:

_____

_____

_____

_____Zip_____

_____

_____

_____

_____Zip_____

*Xerographic copies, hardbound in blue cloth with title and author's name stamped in gold on spine, are available at $2.25 extra.

X-1341/568   Printed in U.S.A.

Fig. 24. Order form for dissertations from University Microfilms

9/International Interlibrary Loan Procedure for United States Libraries

Except for occasional difficulties with Canadian custom restrictions, loans within North America are conducted on the same basis as domestic loans. The CLA and ALA interlibrary loan codes are similar and a similar four-part form is used in both countries.

Interlibrary loans between European countries are governed by the IFLA International Loan Code (1 October 1954)[1] adopted by the Council of the International Federation of Library Associations at Zagreb in September 1954. The ALA Reference Services Division Interlibrary Loan Committee has issued a statement on "International Interlibrary Loan Procedure for United States Libraries"[2] under the IFLA code.

Time is perhaps the most limiting aspect of effective international loan transactions. Airmail is recommended both for requests, reports, and shipment; the requesting library must be prepared for delays in transit; and the lending library must keep in mind that materials loaned will probably be unavailable to local clientele for a minimum of ten weeks, and probably much longer (six months is not unusual).

BORROWING

1. *Eligibility*. Libraries which have indicated a general willingness to lend abroad are eligible to borrow from abroad.

2. *Placing of Requests*. United States libraries should resort to international loan only after the National Union Catalog has failed to find a domestic location.

A foreign library known to have material not found in the United States or Canada may be addressed directly.

---

[1] See appendix M.
[2] 2d rev., June 1963, available from ALA Headquarters Library.

If no location is known, address a bibliographical center in the country of publication. . . .[3]

Form. The International Loan Request form approved by the IFLA Committee on Union Catalogues and International Loans as revised 1969 is available with French, English, and German text (see figure 25);[4] the printing of the form with Russian and English text is to be announced later. The form is in one sheet with a tear-off coupon or counterfoil at the right (perforated). The borrowing library fills out the following portions of the form:

Receipt. Under the IFLA code, the form shall be valid as a receipt provided that the note to this effect has not been crossed out. Most libraries will probably decide to abide by this provision and not cross out.

Author–Title–Place and date. Follow the instructions given in chapter 3, pages 28–39.

Order for microfilm or photocopy. If photocopy or microfilm is an acceptable alternative to the borrowing library, the form preferred should be checked. If cost estimate only is desired, it should be indicated; however, requesting an estimate will considerably delay the filling of the request.

Date–Signature. Date should follow the format: 31/Oct/70. In addition to the signature of the individual responsible for sending the request, the name and title should be typed on the form.

Lent to. Full address, including U.S.A.

Bibliographical verification. Follow instructions given in chapter 3, pages 20–22. Observations and remarks of the borrowing library may be noted in this space.

If not available please forward to. The borrowing library should leave this space blank. It is for the use of the bibliographical center or the lending library.

In writing to a library directly, send one copy of the IFLA International Loan Request form, filled in as specified, with a self-addressed shipping label.

---

[3]See Leendert Brummel and E. Egger, *Guide to Union Catalogues and International Loan Centers,* published under the auspices of IFLA (The Hague: Nijhoff, 1961).

[4]The English-French-German version is available for sale from J. Jorgensen & Co., 40, Artillerivej, DK—2300 Copenhagen S. with name and address of the library printed: 0,07 Danish kroner a copy, (not less than 1,000 copies); without printing, 0,05 Danish kroner a copy. Add mailing costs.

DEMANDE DE PRET INTERNATIONAL INTERNATIONAL LOAN REQUEST BESTELLUNGEN IM INTERNATIONALEN LEIHVERKEHR	Quittance Receipt Quittung

Auteur (ou titre du période., vol., année) - Titre (avec auteur de l'art. du période. et pages) - Lieu et date Author (or periodical title, vol., year) - Title (with author, pages for periodical article) - Place and date Verfasser (oder Titel d. Ztschr., Bd., Jahr) - Titel (mit Verf. u. Seiten f. Ztschr.-Artikel) - Verlagsort u. Jahr	Co'e - Call number - Signatur
L'Enfer. (par Michel Carrouges, etc.) Paris: Ed. de la Revue dex Jeunes, 1950.	Nombre de volumes - Number of volumes - Anzahl der Bände
	Prêté le - Lent on Ausgeliehen am

Commande de microfilm ou de photocopie Order for microfilm or photocopy Bestellung von Mikrofilm oder Photokopie	Remarques et réponses au verso - Observations and replies over-leaf - Bemerkungen und Antworten auf der Rückseite

Microfilm [XX]   Devis
              Cost estimate
              Kostenvoranschlag [ ]
 	
Photocopie [ ]   Si exclu du prêt
              If not available
              Wenn nicht ausleihbar [XX]
	22 Feb. 196 9 Signature - Unterschrift
	
	Sarah Katharine Thomson,
	Library Director

Vérification bibliographique - Bibliographical verification - Bibliographische Angaben

Biblio, 1950, p.264
Bulletin Critique du Livre Francaise, 1950, p.404.

Remarks: U. S. Library of Congress NUC unable to supply
     U. S. locations. If not available in your library,
     please forward.

Si pas disponible, faire circuler à: - If not available please forward to: - Wenn nicht verfügbar, bitte weiterleiten an:

Prêté jusqu'au Lent until Leihfrist bis	Nombre de volumes Number of volumes Anzahl der Bände	Prêté jusqu'au Lent until Leihfrist bis	Nombre de volumes Number of volumes Anzahl der Bände
Cote - Call number - Signatur		Cote - Call number - Signatur	

Timbre de la bibliothèque prêteuse
Stamp of the lending library
Stempel der ausleihenden Bibliothek

Frais de port - Cost of postage
Auslagen für die Post

Valeur déclarée - Value - Wert

Prêté selon le Règlement du prêt international de la FIAB
(1. 10. 1954)
Lent according to the IFLA International Loan Code (1. 10. 1954)
Ausgeliehen gemäss den IFLA-Vorschriften für den
internationalen Leihverkehr (1. 10. 1954)

Seulement à la salle de lecture
Only for reference room
Nur für Lesesaal

Prêté à - Lent to - Ausgeliehen an
Bergen Community College Library
400 Paramus Rd.
Paramus, New Jersey 07652
U. S. A.

Prêté à - Lent to - Ausgeliehen an
Bergen Community Col. Library
400 Paramus Road
Paramus, New Jersey 07652
U. S. A.

Ce talon est à joindre à l'envoi et au retour de l'ouvrage
This counterfoil should be enclosed with the work on its dispatch and on its return
Dieser Abschnitt ist der Sendung wie auch der Rücksendung beizulegen

Commande à exécuter jusqu'au
If the order is not executed till
Falls Bestellung nicht erledigt bis

sinon, renvoyer ce bulletin
please return this lending form
Bestellschein zurücksenden

Fig. 25. IFLA international loan request form, 1969

The envelope should be addressed *Demande de pret International,* Intertional Loan Request, or *Bestellungen im internationalen Leihverkehr* as appropriate. Requests should be sent by airmail.

In writing to a national bibliographical center or union catalog, send two copies of the form, with the lending library's address left blank, and a covering letter asking the center to forward one copy to the library listed as having the title desired and to return the other with that library's name and address added. A self-addressed shipping label should be enclosed as usual.

Notice of shipment and return is not normally made by foreign libraries. The lending library will fill out the coupon or counterfoil portion of the request form and place it in the book. The counterfoil should be preserved and sent back in the book upon its return. If air shipment has been requested, reimbursement in International Reply Coupons of the Universal Postal Union should be sent; photocopies may usually be paid for by bank draft, as specified by the supplying institution.

LENDING

Libraries outside the Western Hemisphere wishing to borrow out-of-print United States books from libraries in the United States may address directly a library known to have the title and known to engage in international loan. If no location is known, they should send requests in duplicate, with the lending library's name and address left blank, to:

> Loan Division
> Library of Congress
> Washington, D.C. 20540
> U.S.A.

Self-addressed shipping labels (see appendix B) should accompany the request.

The Library of Congress will forward one request form and shipping label to the library listed in the unpublished part of the National Union Catalog as having the title. It will return to the requesting library the duplicate form, indicating to which library the request has been forwarded; if there are several locations, the Library of Congress will select one and note as many as two others for use in case the first library to which the request is sent is unable to make the loan. If no location is found in the National Union Catalog, the Library of Congress will, if possible, make the loan itself.

In sending the requested title, the lending library encloses the counterfoil portion of the IFLA request form in the book itself, appropriately filled out, and a self-addressed shipping label for return shipment. Lending libraries should consult the latest edition of the United States Post Office Department's *Directory of International Mail* particularly with regard to weight and height limits for various countries, registration, dissertation and manuscript regulations, airmail, insurance, and marking. Packages should be marked: *BOOKS,* international loans between libraries (International Agreement of 1 October 1954).

Libraries in the United States that are willing to lend to libraries abroad are asked to notify the Loan Division of the Library of Congress, or the chairman of the ALA RSD Interlibrary Loan Committee.

Appendixes

LIBRARY PHOTODUPLICATION ORDER FORM

A

Date of request: September 15, 1969

Requester's Order No. 23145

Supplier's Order No. ....

Call-No.

INTERLIBRARY LOAN LIBRARIAN
BERGEN COMMUNITY COLLEGE
400 PARAMUS ROAD
PARAMUS, NEW JERSEY   07652

REPORTS:
NOT SENT BECAUSE:
☐ Not owned by Library
☐ File is incomplete
☐ In use
   ☐ Hold Placed
   ☐ Request again

☐ Publication not yet received
☐ Please verify your reference
☐ Other:
☐ Suggest you request of:

Estimated Cost of Microfilm ....
                  Photoprint ....

☐ Please pay in advance
☐ Please do not pay in advance

Author (or Periodical title, vol. and year)

American Microscopical Society. Transactions. v.87,Oct.1968
Fold →

Title (with Author and pages for periodical articles) (incl. edition, place and date)

Larsen, J.R. "The neurosecretory cells of the brain of
Aedes aegypti." pages 395–410   ☐ Any edition

Verified in (or Source of reference)

TM January, 1969, p.495; located through ULS
Request ☐ microfilm ☒ photoprint ☐ Other Remarks:

Photographic Services
New York Public Library
Fifth Avenue at 42nd Street
New York, New York 10018

Please send cost estimate for
☐ microfilm   ☐ photoprint

Go ahead with the order if it does not
   exceed: $. 5.00

Special instructions: Please charge to
our deposit account. Thank you.

Jane Smith, Libn.

NOTE: This material is requested in accordance with the A. L. A. recommendations concerning the photocopying of copyrighted materials.

ORDER AUTHORIZED BY:

← Fold

Fold

INTERLIBRARY LOAN   **LIBRARY RATE:**

TO:

**INTERLIBRARY LOAN LIBRARIAN
BERGEN COMMUNITY COLLEGE**
400 PARAMUS ROAD
PARAMUS, NEW JERSEY 07652

Return Requested

...........Parcel post   ....Express collect
...........Preinsured   ....Express prepaid
$........................Value

DEMCO

FROM:

LIBRARY RATE

TO:

Library
Bergen Community College
400 Paramus Road
Paramus, New Jersey 07652

FROM:

Return Requested

...........Parcel post   ....Express collect
...........Preinsured   ....Express prepaid
$........................Value

DEMCO

Shipping labels

INTERLIBRARY LOAN APPLICATION FOR BOOK, PAMPHLET, DISSERTATION, ETC. DATE_____

Author's last name_____First names_____

Title_____

Any edition_____Place_____Publisher_____DATE_____

Series_____

Source of reference, with vol. and page._____

Reader's name_____Status_____Dept_____

Address_____Tel_____

Approved by faculty advisor_____Dept_____

VERIFIED IN   LOCAL LIBRARIES   LOCATIONS: REQUEST DATE
        Year   Vol Page TELEPHONED: NUC Query #_____

LC_____
NUC_____
LC Subj_____
CBI_____
BIP_____
AmDocDiss_____
BM_____
_____

Interlibrary loan workslip for books, pamphlets, dissertations, master's essays, non-serial government documents, and technical reports. Borrowing libraries will adapt to their requirements.

PERIODICAL ARTICLE, AND OTHER SERIALS REQUEST   Date_____

Periodical_____

Vol_____Date_____Pages_____Place of Pub_____

Author and Title of Article_____

_____

Source of Reference_____

Reader's Name_____Status_____Dept_____

Address_____Tel_____

Approval of Faculty Advisor_____Dept_____

VERIFIED IN: Article as well as title MUST be verified.
        Year Vol Page   LOCAL LIBRARIES   LOCATIONS: Date ordered:
  Local union list   _____   TELEPHONED:

ULS_____ _____ _____
NST_____ _____ _____
CA_____ _____ _____
BA_____ _____ _____
IM_____ _____ _____
NOM_____ _____ _____
MLA_____ _____ _____
_____ _____ _____

Interlibrary loan workslip for periodical articles, transactions, proceedings, newspapers on microfilm, and serial government documents. Borrowing libraries will adapt to their requirements.

WORKSLIP CHECKLIST

This is a checklist of items to consider including on your interlibrary loan workslip; since needs of libraries differ, each will want to compose its own; for explanation of the use of this workslip, see page 20. The workslip is filled out by the reader applying for an interlibrary loan, and is used by the library staff when verifying and locating the item, and to type the interlibrary loan request form.

a. BOOK:

    1) Author: last name, first names
    2) Title
    3) Edition; would another edition be satisfactory?
    4) Place, Publisher, and date
    5) Series
    6) For Theses and Dissertations: Degree, University, and date

b. PERIODICAL:

    1) Name of periodical
    2) Volume
    3) Date
    4) Author of article
    5) Title of article
    6) Pagination

c. PRINTED SOURCE OF REFERENCE with full citation

d. READER

    1) Reader's full name
    2) Status and Department
    3) Address and Telephone Number
    4) Purpose of loan
    5) Not wanted after _____.
    6) Photocopy or microfilm acceptable? Agrees to payment if less than $_____.
    7) Substitute acceptable?
    8) Approved by faculty advisor: Name, Rank and Department.

e. VERIFICATION including pagination, volume, and date

f. LIBRARY LOCATIONS

REPLY FORM FOR NON-CIRCULATING THESES AND DISSERTATIONS

―――

Interlibrary Loan Service
ANYWHERE UNIVERSITY LIBRARY
300 BROAD STREET
Anywhere, U. S. 00000

THE THESIS YOU REQUESTED IS NOT AVAILABLE FOR LOAN:

_____ It is our only copy.

_____ Master's essays prior to 1935, and Ed.D. and Ph.D. theses
prior to 1920 do not circulate.

_____ This department can supply photocopy or microfilm. The thesis
is approximately _____pages. Please see separate price
list. Do not send payment with order; you will be billed for
the exact amount. Orders should be sent to the address above.
Please give full author, title, degree, and year.

_____ Ph.D. theses beginning June, 1954, are available only from:
University Microfilms
300 North Zeeb Road
Ann Arbor, Michigan 48106
Dissertation Abstracts, volume_____page_____ gives the
following order information for this thesis:
Author_____
UM Order number_____
Positive 35mm microfilm price_____
Xerographic copy price_____
Do not send payment with order; you will be billed at the
time of shipment, plus handling and shipping charges and
taxes where applicable.

SAMPLE REPLY TO INADEQUATE REQUESTS

Interlibrary Loan Service
BERGEN COMMUNITY COLLEGE LIBRARY
400 Paramus Road
Paramus, New Jersey 07652

Telephone 201-447-1500, x18 or 19.

Please note that this request, as indicated below, does not meet
the requirements of the National Interlibrary Loan Code, 1968,
and the Interlibrary Loan Procedure Manual, published by the
American Library Association. We are filling the request. In
the future we could give you faster, more accurate service if you
would follow these instructions.

We regret that we must return the enclosed loan request(s). The
reason   it has   not been processed is checked below. Please
correct the request form as suggested and return it to us for
processing. Consult the Interlibrary Loan Procedure Manual
published by the American Library Association.

____ Please submit requests, typed, on ALA Interlibrary Loan Request forms.

____ Please list only one title per form.

____ Please verify your citation, , and give source, volume and page where
found. If unable to verify, source of reference should always be
indicated.

____ Citation is incomplete: please indicate:

_____ Full names of author

_____ Main entry in full, do not abbreviate

_____ Complete title

_____ Date of publication

_____ Volume

_____ Pagination of article

_____ Author and title of periodical article.

____ Please verify location before sending requests.

____ The request should be signed by the librarian responsible for interlibrary loan requests.

____ Please type the full name and address of the borrowing library in the
upper box.

THE LIBRARY OF CONGRESS
REFERENCE DEPARTMENT
LOAN DIVISION

INTERLIBRARY LOAN

Under the system of interlibrary loans the Library of Congress will lend certain books *to other libraries* for the use of investigators engaged in serious research. The loan will rest on the theory of a special service to scholarship which is not within the power or the duty of the local or regional library to render. Its purpose is to aid research calculated to advance the boundaries of knowledge, by the loan of unusual books not readily accessible elsewhere. It is organized to complement the resources of other libraries, but not to supply the major part of the materials needed for any extended research. Consequently, it does not contemplate, nor its scope extend to, loans of large numbers of items required for use in a single investigation.

The material lent cannot include, therefore:

(*a*) Books that should be available from a local or regional library (such as a State library) having a particular duty to the area from which the application comes.

(*b*) Books that are in print and procurable through ordinary trade channels.

(*c*) Books for the general reader, textbooks, or popular manuals.

(*d*) Books for student or study club work, or the preparation of a thesis.

(*e*) Books in constant use in Washington, the loan of which would be an inconvenience to Congress, or to other Government agencies, or to reference readers in the Library of Congress. These conditions would ordinarily exclude from this loan system many official documents, books in the several reference collections, language dictionaries, and encyclopedias.

(*f*) Newspapers and periodicals.

(*g*) Genealogies and United States local and State histories.

(*h*) Sheet music and librettos.

(*i*) Motion picture films.

(*j*) Phonograph and language records.

(*k*) Books in the Rare Book Collections.

(*l*) Manuscripts.

(*m*) Volumes in poor physical condition.

(*n*) Material which by reason of its size or its character requires expensive packing or high insurance.

Requests for loans should be addressed to the Chief, Loan Division, Library of Congress, Washington, D. C. 20540. Loans are made for a period of two weeks from the date of receipt. One extension for a like period will be granted upon request, whenever feasible. Customarily, loans to college and university libraries are limited to books required by faculty members for use in their personal researches.

Music (except in certain cases such as unbound music, manuscripts, first editions, rare volumes, or parts for orchestral or chamber music works) is lent on the same conditions as books. Musical scores so lent, however, may not be used for performances, but for reference and study only.

The borrowing library must assume complete responsibility for the safety and prompt return of all material borrowed. It is expected to apply to the material borrowed the same safeguards it would apply to material of its own, requiring to be used on its premises any material that it would not itself lend for use outside. The borrowing library is expected also, in cases of loss or damage, to attend to details of making replacements.

Subject to the limitations indicated above, the Library of Congress welcomes applications for loans coming properly within the intent and purpose of the system. It must emphasize, however, that its ability to deal promptly and effectively with such requests will often depend upon the clearness and specification of the applications. Those applications which require research to identify the material requested or to select items responsive to a need must yield precedence to explicit requests for particular works.

Photoreproductions of materials in the collections of the Library of Congress are available at moderate cost. The filling of an order for photoreproduction is dependent on availability of the material in the Library of Congress, and on written permission from the copyright owner in the case of copyrighted material. Send your request, including complete bibliographic data, to: *Chief, Photoduplication Service, Library of Congress*, Washington, D. C. 20540.

U.S. GOVERNMENT PRINTING OFFICE

THE LIBRARY OF CONGRESS

WASHINGTON, D. C. 20540

REFERENCE DEPARTMENT
LOAN DIVISION

Dear Librarian:

The interlibrary loan service of the Library of Congress has been extended to include the occasional loan of unusual books for the use of doctoral candidates under the following conditions:

1. The materials requested are supplementary to the university library's resources; the student can rely on these resources for the major part of his doctoral dissertation needs; and the Library of Congress would not be expected to furnish more than an occasional item to any one student.

2. The materials requested are not in the categories which the Library of Congress does not lend; e.g., rare books, books in print, etc.

3. The requesting library will note on its request that it has exhausted all possible resources before requesting the loan.

4. That consideration has been given to purchasing a photocopy and that the loan of the original is requested only when photocopying is not feasible because of expense, nature of materials, or similar valid reasons.

The Library of Congress is happy to be able to augment the body of research materials available to scholars who are unable to use material here; however, the privilege may have to be withdrawn if the volume of requests becomes too great for the Loan Division to handle.

Sincerely yours,

Legare H. B. Obear
Chief of Loan Division

THE LIBRARY OF CONGRESS

WASHINGTON, D. C. 20540

ADMINISTRATIVE DEPARTMENT
PHOTODUPLICATION SERVICE

Date_____

        Thank you for your enclosed inquiry. Since we have not
retained a copy of your request, <u>if you write us concerning it, please
be sure to return all of these papers</u>. Our report is indicated by one
or more of the following notations or other comments written on the
margins of your request.

_____Bind - In bindery; renew your request in 30 days.

_____(C) - Copyrighted; photocopies can be supplied only if you
            resubmit your order together with written permission of
            the copyright owner whose name and address are shown below.

_____Cat - Being cataloged; renew your request in 30 days.

_____LC° - Not located as cited in the Library of Congress collections.

_____Loan - On loan; renew your request in 30 days.

_____NI - Not identified as cited. If additional information is
           furnished, we will search again.

_____NOS - Not on shelf; renew your request in 30 days.

_____Ref - The institution(s) indicated below is/are listed as having
           the material; you may wish to refer your request to them.

_____TB - Tightly bound; some loss or distortion of text may occur.
         Please confirm your order.

_____TFTC - Too fragile to copy.

_____TRPL - Title received; part lacking.

_____Mfm - Being microfilmed; if positive microfilm or photocopy is
          acceptable, renew your request in 90 days.

NATIONAL LIBRARY OF MEDICINE
8600 Rockville Pike
Bethesda, Maryland 20014

Interlibrary Loan Policy (Revised April 1970)

Most of the literature in the collection of the National Library of Medicine
is available for loan to any library, with the exception of ordinary current,
trade publications for which the presumption of widespread availability is
reasonable. Requests for reprints should be directed to the author.

Readers who cannot obtain medical literature in their Regions and who cannot
come to the National Library of Medicine in person may secure material through
the interlibrary loan service of the Library by applying through their Regional
Medical Library or local resource library. Loans from NLM are made subject to
compliance with the following regulations and instructions and the provisions
of the National Interlibrary Loan Code of the American Library Association.
Only a few requests should be submitted at one time from any library or for
any one patron.

FORM OF LOANS

1. The National Library of Medicine reserves the right to determine
whether material will be lent in the original form or as a photoduplicate.

2. Photoduplicates sent instead of original material will be supplied
without charge to libraries in the United States. Photoduplicates may be
retained permanently by the borrowing library, unless return is specifically
requested by NLM.

3. With sufficient justification, NLM may lend complete issues or
volumes of serials when such loan does not impair other service, but in no
case will complete issues or volumes or substantial portions of issues or
volumes be copied as a loan. Photocopies will be limited to no more than one
article per issue and three articles per volume from any journal. Multiple
copies will not be furnished.

4. Original material will not be lent outside the United States.

METHOD OF BORROWING

1. Borrowing libraries will submit typed requests on the Interlibrary
Loan Request Form approved by the American Library Association, or by TWX.
Requests made by letter or on other forms cannot be processed and will be
returned to the sender. Each item or item segment must be requested on a
separate form.

2. Each request must be authenticated, in handwriting, by authorized
personnel in the borrowing library. Unsigned requests will be returned.

3. Libraries are expected to avail themselves of the resources of their
Region rather than directing requests to NLM. Resource or Regional Medical
Libraries which are unable to fill requests will forward them to NLM for
processing.

CITATIONS

1. Citations should be complete. Periodical references should contain name of the journal, date of issue, volume number, author, title, and pagination of article. Reference to books should include full name of author, title, edition, place, publisher, and date, in the space designated on the Interlibrary Loan Request Form.

2. References should be verified before they are submitted. Incorrect references will not be verified by this Library unless the borrowing library has exhausted its bibliographic resources, in which case notation to that effect, and summary of sources searched, should be furnished on the form.

3. If a reference cannot be verified by the requesting library, the bibliographic citation to its source should be given.

LOAN PERIOD

1. The borrowing library may retain original material for four weeks from date of its receipt at the library unless a shorter period is specified.

2. An original volume loaned by NLM may be recalled at any time.

3. Renewal for two weeks may be granted if the renewal request is received prior to the due date. No renewal will be granted if the request is received after the due date.

DELIVERY AND RETURNS

1. All loans will be sent out by NLM with postage prepaid.

2. The borrowing library should take great care in packing original volumes for return to NLM. Corners and edges of books should be well protected; unbound material should not be rolled, but should be sent flat.

3. The borrowing library will pay postage costs for the return of loans of original volumes.

4. Borrowing libraries are responsible for original volumes from the time they receive them until the volumes are returned to NLM and received there. Materials lost during that interval must be replaced by the borrowing library. For the protection of the borrower, books should be insured while in transit.

SPECIAL PHOTOGRAPHIC SERVICES

1. Special photographic procedures are required to copy some items in the collection, and a charge will be made for this service. Cost estimates are available on request. NLM will consider requests for copying items such as portraits, photographs, and other pictorial work as facilities allow. Advance payment is required for this work. In general, rapid service on these requests is not available.

2. Orders for materials protected by copyright will not be accepted for special photographic service unless accompanied by written permission from the copyright owner.

ACCESS TO ARTICLES CITED

Users of Index Medicus who wish to consult the articles cited are advised to utilize the following sources:

1. Reprints of the articles are frequently available directly from the author or publisher.

2. Medical libraries in local university medical centers, medical schools, health centers, hospitals, and state or county medical societies will often have the material on hand, or by means of union lists know where it can be obtained through interlibrary loan.

3. Special libraries or libraries of national associations in the various fields of medicine can provide much of the literature that is indexed.

4. If your librarian cannot obtain the material through interlibrary loan elsewhere, the loan request may be directed to Regional Medical Libraries which will accept requests from libraries in their Region, forwarding to the National Library of Medicine those requests which they are unable to fill.

SAMPLE BORROWING POLICY FOR DISTRIBUTION TO READERS

WASHINGTON UNIVERSITY
John M. Olin Library

INTERLIBRARY LOAN SERVICE

Interlibrary loan service is offered through the Reference Department to faculty
members and to graduate students who are engaged in research. The conditions of
this service are set by the Interlibrary Loan Code of the American Library
Association and by regulations of individual lending libraries.

This library depends for loans upon the larger American research libraries which
carry a heavy interlibrary loan burden. We can make them no commensurate return.
Potential borrowers should keep this in mind and ask only for necessary materials
which can be obtained in no other way.

ELIGIBILITY FOR LOANS

In accordance with the practice of research libraries, faculty members and
graduate students engaged in thesis research are eligible for loans. Materials
available in local libraries will be borrowed for graduate students who are not
eligible for general interlibrary loan privileges; other materials they request
will automatically be purchased, on a rush basis, rather than borrowed. If the
original is not in print, a microfilm copy will be purchased.

LIMITATIONS ON LOANS

The following types of materials cannot ordinarily be requested: (NOTE: for
alternative methods of obtaining them see below, under SUBSTITUTES FOR LOANS)

1. Materials for class use
2. A high percentage of books basic for a thesis
3. American books in print (except for books available in local libraries)
4. Periodicals
5. Materials which are difficult and expensive to pack
6. Reference books
7. Rare Books
8. Dissertations which are available for purchase in the form of photocopies
9. Books owned by this library and temporarily in use
10. Material which has been recently borrowed and returned

DURATION OF LOANS

The time allowed by the lending library is indicated on a slip inserted in the
book. An extension of time should be requested only in unusual circumstances.
Application for such renewal must be made before the date indicated on the date
due slip. If a borrower continually disregards due dates, he may be refused
further service.

RESTRICTIONS ON USE

This library is bound by any restrictions on use imposed by the lending library.
Some libraries require that the materials they lend be used in the borrowing library. Some require the signatures of the readers of unpublished dissertations.

The borrower should not let others use the books he secures on loan unless
special arrangements have been made. No photocopying should be done without
permission.

SUBSTITUTES FOR LOANS

If materials requested cannot be obtained on interlibrary loan, they will be automatically purchased on a rush basis (either in the original or in photocopy).

Dissertations available on microfilm will be purchased since in most cases they are not available for loan. Graduate students are asked to secure authorization from their advisers before the order is placed. The dissertation will be added to the library's collection if it seems appropriate.

In many cases periodical articles will be purchased in photocopy since most libraries no longer lend periodicals. The copy will be given to the person requesting the loan.

INTERLIBRARY LOAN INSTRUCTIONS

1. Fill out an application form for each item requested, a green form for a periodical, a white one for a book. (A supply of forms is kept at the Reference Desk.) Indicate on this form all the information necessary to identify the work. In the case of periodicals and other serial publications this includes author and title of article, title of serial, volume, date, and complete pagination of article; in the case of books, author, title, place of publication, publisher and date. If full information cannot be provided, a complete citation to the place where the reference was found is essential.

2. Leave your application at the Reference Desk. You will be notified when the material is received. Unless it is available in a local library you may ordinarily expect to wait at least two weeks. If no locations are known, an inquiry must be sent to the Union Catalog at the Library of Congress, and this may cause further delay.

3. As soon as possible after receipt of notification of the material's arrival it should be called for at the Reference Desk. Books may be taken from the building unless there is a note on the date due slip indicating the contrary; if the borrower does not have to return the material (in the case of photocopies) a note to this effect is written on the date due slip.

4. Return borrowed material to the Reference Desk as soon as you have finished with it; it <u>must</u> be returned by the due date.

November, 1967

SAMPLE POLICY FOR LENDING TO REPRINTERS

<u>ACCESS TO COLUMBIA UNIVERSITY LIBRARY MATERIAL BY REPRINT PUBLISHERS</u>

<u>Policy</u>

The Columbia University Libraries will consider requests from publishers for the loan of specific titles for reprinting purposes. If the title is judged to be one that can be made available for reprinting or editorial review, the volume(s) will be loaned under conditions that will safeguard the Libraries' collections, protect library users, and recover all costs incurred.

<u>Practice</u>

The conditions for loan are these:

1. A service charge of $5.00 will be made for every title borrowed by a publisher, whether for reprinting purposes, for editorial review or for copying one or a few pages. If volumes of a serial are borrowed at various times, there will be a $5.00 service charge for each group borrowed.

2. A reprint privilege fee of $25.00 will be charged for (1) each monograph volume and (2) for each numbered volume of a serial actually reprinted.

3. One copy of the reprint will be provided as soon as it is available.

4. Volumes borrowed for editorial use or for photographing a few pages will be returned in the same physical condition as when they were borrowed. Loans for these purposes will be for as brief a period as possible, with a maximum of one month.

5. Volumes borrowed for reprinting will be returned with a minimum of delay, regardless of their physical condition. Volumes are to be returned unbound.

Publishers wishing to use Columbia materials should write to:

James E. Fall
Assistant Head of Acquisitions
231 Butler Library
Columbia University
New York, New York 10027

Richard H. Logsdon
Director of Libraries

July 1, 1966

OKLAHOMA TELETYPE INTERLIBRARY SYSTEM REQUEST

A   REPORTED ON OTIS

OTIS FILLS THE GAP

REPORTS: CHECKED BY _____

SENT-BOOK RATE _____

☐ OTHER _____ INSURED FOR $_____

DATE SENT _____ CHARGES $_____

LOAN PERIOD _____ (FOR PERIOD OF LOAN)

☐ FOR USE IN LIBRARY ONLY

NOT SENT BECAUSE:

☐ NOT OWNED BY LIBRARY
☐ NON-CIRCULATING
☐ IN USE
☐ OTHER
☐ SUGGESTED OTHER SOURCE
☐ HOLD PLACED
☐ REQUEST AGAIN
☐ ESTIMATED COST OF PHOTOPRINT $_____

RECORDS: FOR BORROWING LIBRARY

DATE RECEIVED _____

DATE RETURNED _____

☐ BY BOOK RATE   ☐ OTHER

INSURANCE $_____

RENEWAL REQUEST:

REQUESTED ON _____

RENEWAL DATE _____ (OR PERIOD OF RENEWAL)

This sample teletype request form is in two parts, which can serve as either A, Request, and D, Notice of Return, for the borrowing library or as A, Request, and B, Report, for the lending library. The forms are in rolls, are punched in the margins for continuous feed in the teletypewriter, and are perforated for separating. NCR paper in two- and three-copy rolls that do not require sprocketing the teletypewriter are also generally available.

IFLA INTERNATIONAL LOAN CODE (1 October 1954)[1]

I. *Object*

The international lending system, organized under the auspices of IFLA sets out to give libraries taking part in the scheme the opportunity to bring from abroad by the surest, quickest and most economical route works that are indispensable for certain research and are not available in their own country.

II. *Membership*

Libraries which formally accept the present rules and are prepared to grant full reciprocity to other libraries taking part in the scheme, are considered to be members of the international lending system. The Secretariat of IFLA (c/o United Nations Library, Geneva) will accept requests for admission through the national centre of each country (cf. Ch. III, I) or, alternatively, through the association, or one of the associations, of librarians in the country concerned. Libraries not authorized to grant full reciprocal facilities may nevertheless join the international lending system if their national centre undertakes to have books requested from abroad sent by other libraries in tne country.

The Secretariat of IFLA will publish periodical lists of libraries taking part in the international lending system.

---

[1] The French text of the IFLA International Loan Code was printed in <u>Libri</u> 4, no. 2:168-170, 1954. The English text appeared in <u>UNESCO Bulletin for Libraries</u> 9:5-6, January 1955.

III. *Organization*

1. It is recommended that a national centre for the international lending system be set up in each country, and that this centre shall maintain contact with a large library and shall include, if possible, a union catalogue and an information service.

The task of the national centre shall be: (a) to forward requests from abroad to libraries in its country belonging to the international lending system and having, or being likely to have in their possession the volumes asked for; (b) to check requests made by its country, ensure that the books asked for are not already available in one of its country's libraries and, if they are not to be found, to send on the request abroad; (c) to draw up, with the assistance of libraries in its country (cf. Ch. III,9) statistics of international loans they have effected and to send these figures annually to the Secretariat of IFLA.

2. The borrowing library shall bear the full cost of sending and forwarding books for which it has asked. From the moment the books are despatched, the borrowing library shall be responsible in case of loss, and for any damage they may suffer. National centres and libraries are recommended to forgo, on a reciprocal basis, the repayment of forwarding costs. If repayment is nevertheless demanded, it shall preferably be made when the works borrowed have been returned.

3. All requests shall be made on the form adopted by IFLA.[2] This form shall be drawn up in French or in the national language accompanied by a French translation. The borrowing library shall verify and, if necessary, complete as far as possible the bibliographical references

_____

[2]See figure 25 and page 67.

of works requested and shall note them on the back of the form.

4. The form shall be valid as a receipt provided that the note to this effect has not been crossed out.

5. Loans shall normally be made for one month excluding the time required for the despatch and return of the works requested. The library making the loan may, however, extend or curtail this time-limit.

6. Works shall be consulted in accordance with the rules of the library requesting them, unless the library making the loan decides otherwise.

7. Each library shall be free to decide whether it agrees or refuses to lend a work that has been asked for. For rare or valuable works the library may demand special guarantees.

As a general rule the following types of publication shall not be sent: (a) works excluded from outside loan; (b) publications on sale in bookshops at less than the equivalent of 5 Swiss francs or $1 (U.S.A.).

Books which are to be found in the country served by the national centre, but which are momentarily on loan, shall not be requested through the international lending system. Manuscripts shall, as far as possible, be loaned under the same conditions as printed matter.

8. Forms and parcels shall normally be sent through the post. The diplomatic bag shall not be used, in view of the delays attendant on this method. The despatch counterfoil (right-hand part of the form) shall be sent with the volume on the outward and on the return journey. Packages shall be marked as follows: *Books,* international loan between libraries (International Agreement of 1 October 1954).

9. Libraries taking part in the international lending system shall keep statistics of volumes lent and requested and shall send this record

every year to the national centre or to their national association, for forwarding to the Secretariat of IFLA.

10. In the case of volumes excluded from international lending efforts shall be made to procure photocopies and microfilms. The national centre shall, if possible, have at its disposal a reproduction service for supplying such copies on behalf of libraries not equipped for this purpose. The national centre must also be in a position to indicate libraries and centres having reproduction services. The cost of making photocopies shall be charged to the library ordering them

IV.   *The IFLA Committee on Union Catalogues and International Loans*[3]

This committee shall study all questions relating to the international lending system. It is the only body competent to submit to the IFLA Council recommendations for the development and extension of this form of international library co-operation.

---

[3]As of release of June 1, 1969:
Chairman: Torben Nielsen,   Secretary: Carlo Hury
           University Library,   Bibliotheque nationale,
           Humanities Section   14a, Boulevard royal
           1, Fiolstraede,   LUXEMBOURG-Ville
           DK - 1171 COPENHAGEN K.

STANDARD ABBREVIATIONS OF SOURCES OF VERIFICATION

Agricultural Index	Ag I
Air University Library Index to Military Periodicals	Air U Mil Per
American Doctoral Dissertations	Am Doc Diss
L'Année Philologique	Ann Philol
Applied Science and Technology Index	ASTI
Art Index	Art I
Avery Index to Architectural Periodicals	Avery I
Biblio	Biblio
Bibliografía General Española e Hispano-americana	Bib Esp
Bibliografía Hispánica	Bib Hisp
Bibliographie de la France	Bib Fr
Bibliographie der Deutschen Zeitschriftenliteratur	IBZ - A
Bibliographie der fremdsprachigen Zeitschriften-literatur	IBZ - B
Bibliographie Géographique Internationale	Bib Geog Int
Bibliography and Index of Geology Exclusive of North America	Bib I Geol
Bibliography of Agriculture	Bib Ag
Bibliography of Asian Studies	Bib Asian Stud
Bibliography of North American Geology	Bib NA Geol
Bibliothèque Nationale. Paris. Catalogue Général	BN
Biography Index	Biog I
Biological Abstracts	BA
Biological and Agricultural Index	Biol Ag
Book Review Digest	BRD
Books in Print	BIP
Botanical Abstracts	Bot A

Botanisches Zentralblatt	Bot Z
Brinkman's Catalogus van Boeken	Brinkman
British Books in Print	BBIP
British Museum. General Catalogue of Printed Books	BM
British National Bibliography	BNB
British Union-Catalogue of Periodicals	BUCOP
Bulletin signalétique	Bull Sig
Business Periodicals Index	BPI
Cambridge Bibliography of English Literature	CBEL
Catalogo Cumulativo del Bollettino delle Pubblicazioni Italiane	Cat Cum Ital
Chemical Abstracts	CA
Chemisches Zentralblatt	Chem Z
Child Development Abstracts	Child Dev A
Cumulative Book Index	CBI
Cumulative Index to Nursing Literature	CI Nur Lit
Cyrillic Union Catalog [microprint edition]	Cyr Un Cat
Deutsche Nationalbibliographie	Deut Nat bib
Deutsches Bücherverzeichnis	DBV
Dissertation Abstracts	DA
Doctoral Dissertations Accepted by American Universities	Doc Diss
Economic Abstracts	Econ A
Education Index	Ed I
Engineering Index	Engr I
English Catalogue of Books	Eng Cat
Essay and General Literature Index	EGLI
Excerpta Medica	EM
Experiment Station Record	Exp Sta Rec
Geophysical Abstracts	Geophys A
GeoScience Abstracts	GeoS A

Handbook of Latin American Studies	HLAS
Historical Abstracts	Hist A
Index of Economic Journals	I Econ J
Index to Dental Literature	I Dent Lit
Index to Latin American Periodical Literature	I LA per Lit
Index to Latin American Periodicals	I LA Per
Index to Legal Periodicals	I Leg Per
Index Medicus	IM
Index to Religious Periodical Literature	I Rel Per Lit
Industrial Arts Index	Indus Art I
International Aerospace Abstracts	Int Aero A
International Bibliography of Economics	Int Bib Econ
International Bibliography of Historical Sciences	Int Bib Hist Sci
International Bibliography of Political Science	Int Bib Pol Sci
International Bibliography of Social and Cultural Anthropology	Int Bib Anthr
International Bibliography of Sociology	Int Bib Soc
International Catalogue of Scientific Literature	Int Cat Sci Lit
International Congresses and Conferences	Int Cong Conf
International Index	Int I
International Political Science Abstracts	Int Pol Sci A
Internationale Bibliographie der Zeitschriften-literatur	IBZ
Jahres-Verzeichnis der Deutschen Hochschulschriften	Jahr Deut Hoch
Kayser. Vollständiges Bücher-Lexikon	Kayser
Library Literature	Lib Lit
Library of Congress Catalog	LC Cat
Library of Congress. Cumulative Subject Catalog	LC Subj
Library Science Abstracts	Lib Sci A
Libros en venta en Hispanoamérica y España	Lib en venta
List of Periodicals Abstracted by Chemical Abstracts	CA List Per

Lorenz. Catalogue Général de la Librairie Française	Lorenz
Mathematical Reviews	Math R
Meteorological and Geoastrophysical Abstracts	Meteor Geoastr
Modern Language Association. MLA American Bibliography	MLA
Modern Languare Association. MLA International Bibliography	MLA
Monthly Index of Russian Accessions	Mo I Russ Acc
Music Index	Mus I
National Library of Medicine Current Catalog	NLM
National Union Catalog [printed]	NUC
National Union Catalog [on cards at LC]	DLC-UCD
New Serial Titles	NST
New York. Metropolitan Museum of Art Library Catalog	Met Mus Lib Cat
New York Public Library. Dictionary Catalog of the Slavonic Collection	NYPL Slav
Newspapers on Microfilm	NOM
Nuclear Science Abstracts	NSA
Nutrition Abstracts and Reviews	Nutr A
Pagliaini. Catalogo Generale della Libreria Italiana	Pagliani
Palau y Dulcet. Manual del Librero Hispano-americano	Palau
Peabody Museum of Archaeology and Ethnology. Library Author Catalog	Peabody Mus Auth
Peabody Museum of Archaeology and Ethnology. Library Subject Catalog	Peabody Mus Subj
Philosopher's Index	Philos I
Play Index	Play I
Poggendorff. Biographisch-literarisches Hand- wörterbuch	Poggendorff
Poole's Index to Periodical Literature	Poole
Psychological Abstracts	Psych A
Public Affairs Information Service Bulletin	PAIS
Quarterly Cumulative Index Medicus	QCIM

Readers' Guide to Periodical Literature	RG
Religious and Theological Abstracts	Rel Theol A
Répertoire Bibliographique de la Philosophie	Rép Bib Philos
Repertoire d'Art et d'Archéologie	Rép Art
Rome. Centro Nazionale per il Catalogo Unico delle Biblioteche Italiane e per le Informazioni Bibliografiche. Primo Catalogo collettivo delle Biblioteche Italiane.	Prim Cat Col Ital
Royal Society of London. Catalogue of Scientific Papers	Roy Soc Cat
Science Abstracts. A. Physics Abstracts	Sci A-A
B. Electrical Engineering Abstracts	Sci A-B
Scientific and Technical Aerospace Reports	STAR
Serial Publications of Foreign Governments	SPFG
Short Story Index	Short Story I
Social Sciences and Humanities Index	SSHI
Sociological Abstracts	Soc A
Union List of Newspapers	ULN
Union List of Serials	ULS
United Nations Documents Index	UNDI
U. S. Armed Forces Medical Library Catalog	AFML Cat
United States Catalog	U. S. Cat
United States Government Publications; Monthly Catalog	Mo Cat
U. S. Government Research and Development Reports	USGRDR
U. S. Surgeon General's Office. Index-catalogue of the Library	Sur Gen Cat
Vertical File Index	VFI
Water Pollution Abstracts	Water Pol A
World List of Scientific Periodicals	WLSP
Zoological Record	Zool Rec

MAJOR UNION CATALOGS OF THE UNITED STATES AND CANADA

SUMMER, 1968

CALIFORNIA

Union Catalog at the California State Library

Library/Courts Building

P. O. Box 2037

Sacramento, Calif. 95809

Tel 916-445-5730. TWX 910-367-3553. Editor vacant

80 libraries; 1,854,214 cards; 46,264 cards added last year.

Includes: Major public libraries in Calif.

Description: Begun 1909. Main entry cards, some cross references

   and some added entries. No documents, selected juvenile and fiction.

Non-member service: Free to all who request.

COLORADO

Bibliographical Center for Research

Rocky Mountain Region, Inc.

1357 Broadway

Denver, Colorado 80203

Tel 303-266-0851 ex 242. TWX 910-931-0499. Director Phoebe F. Hayes,

70 libraries; 5,000,000 cards; 688,000 cards added 1968.

Includes: Academic, special, state and public libraries in 11 states.

Description: Cards for books, periodicals and newspapers; bibliographies,

   abstracts, and indexes; technical report literature.

Non-member service: Fee schedule available upon request.

DISTRICT OF COLUMBIA

National Union Catalog

Union Catalog Division

Library of Congress

Washington, D. C. 20540

<u>Tel</u> 202-967-8125. <u>TWX</u> 710-822-0185 <u>Chief</u> George A. Schwegmann, Jr.

400 libraries currently report, many more represented; 18,000,000 cards;

   800,000 cards added last year.

Includes: Academic, special, and public libraries.

Description: Cards representing an estimated nine million different

   titles found in L. C. and other major libraries in the U. S. and

   Canada. Main entry, with cross references and added entries for

   joint authors, editors, compilers, etc; no subject approach.

   Includes entries for more important books copied from regional

   union catalogs in Philadelphia, Cleveland, Chapel Hill, N. C.,

   Seattle, and Denver.

The Division also maintains the Microfilm Clearing House and the

control files of <u>Newspapers on Microfilm</u> and the <u>National Register of

Microform Masters</u>, both of which are published by the division.

Serials first issued in 1950 or after are recorded by the Serial Record

Division, and published in <u>New Serial Titles</u>. Practically all mono-

graphic titles published in 1956 or later that are reported by the

major research libraries of the U. S. and Canada are published in

<u>The National Union Catalog, a Cumulative Author List;</u> additional

locations appear in the <u>Register of Additional Locations.</u> The

<u>National Union Catalog Pre-1956 Imprints</u> is being published. Other

Union Catalogs maintained at the Library of Congress include: Chinese,

Japanese, Korean, Hebrew, Yiddish, Slavic, and Cyrillic. Reports to

the National Union Catalog about United Nations, League of Nations,

United States Federal, and U. S. State documents have not been consis-

tent.

Service: There is no membership involved in the use of the National

Union Catalog. The catalog may be consulted in person by members of

the public, and searches for locations of desired books are made in response to requests from libraries and individuals. Because of

limitations in personnel, long lists and lists for commercial firms

cannot be searched. In such instances, inquirers are referred to

competent searchers who will do the work independently at stated

rates.

See Chapter VI for directions for requesting locations from the

National Union Catalog.

GEORGIA

Union Catalogue of the Atlanta-Athens Area

Library Building, Emory University

Atlanta, Georgia 30322

Tel 404-378-2811 Director Dorothy Harbin

28 libraries; 1,100,000 cards; 93, 719 cards added last year.

Includes: Academic, public and special libraries.

Description: Main entry catalog for books and serials. No

   subject entries.

Non-member services: Open to the public. Mail and telephone inquiries

   accepted. There is no fee unless the volume of requests becomes

   so great as to cause a burden on the Catalogue.

NEBRASKA

Nebraska Union Catalog

Nebraska Public Library Commission

State Capitol Building

Lincoln, Nebraska 68509

Tel 402-473-1545. TWX 910-621-8119 Director Mrs. Dorothy W.

   Lessenhop.

28 libraries; 2,424,780 cards; 79,373 cards. added last year.

Includes: Large public, college and university libraries.

Description: Main entry catalog of books and journals.

Non-member services: Reasonable searching, no charge.

NEW HAMPSHIRE

Union List of New Hampshire Libraries

New Hampshire State Library

20 Park Street

Concord, N. H. 03301

Tel 603-271-2144. TWX 710-361-6467 Director Stella J. Scheckter

36 libraries; 292,500 cards; 19,500 cards added last year.

Includes: Public, college and private school libraries.

Description: Main entry catalog of adult non-fiction and foreign
    language books.

Services: Direct borrowing service for N. H. residents and libraries.
    Location service from Union list for out-of-state patrons without fee.

NORTH CAROLINA

North Carolina Interlibrary Center

Louis Round Wilson Library

University of North Carolina

Chapel Hill, North Carolina 27514

Tel 919-933-1326 TWX 510-920-0760 Director Samuel M. Boone

30 active libraries, about 70 others partially represented; 950,000
    cards; 54,323 cards added last year.

Includes: University, college and public libraries.

Description: An attempt to list on cards locations for every adult
    non-fiction title in North Carolina libraries (with such exceptions
    as music scores, theses and government documents).

Non-member service: Location service by mail or TWX to libraries or
    individuals at no cost (as time permits).

OHIO

Cleveland Regional Union Catalog

Case Western Reserve University Library

Cleveland, Ohio 44106

Tel 216-368-3522 Director Arthur D. Mink

30 libraries currently; 3,159,727 cards; 49,083 added last year.

Includes: Public, university and college libraries.

Description: Author catalog of books.

Non-member service: Service given to all without a fee.

Union Catalog of the State Library of Ohio

1434 West Fifth Avenue

Columbus, Ohio 43212

Tel 614-486-7255   Director   Vacant

37 libraries; 3,000,000 cards; 28,954 cards added last year.

Includes: 32 Ohio public libraries, 4 special libraries and the
  State Library of Ohio.

Description: Main entry for adult non-fiction.

Non-member service: Location information supplied to libraries by
  mail or telephone. No fees presently involved (1968).

PENNSYLVANIA

Union Library Catalogue of Pennsylvania

3420 Walnut Street

Philadelphia, Pa. 19104

Tel 215-EV 2-5104 TWX 710-670-3450 Director Eleanor Este Campion

121 active libraries, 91 others partially listed; 3,375,000 cards;
  350,000 cards added last year.

Includes: All important university, college, special, public and
  industrial libraries in the Philadelphia area including the four
  Resource Libraries included in the Pennsylvania Library Plan.

Description. Books and journals.

Non-member service: The Catalogue acts as a back-up service to the
    interlibrary loan requests sent from out-of-state to local libraries.
    As most of its holdings are included in the National Union Catalog,
    and as the Catalogue checks the Weekly List issued by the National
    Union Catalog, it discourages direct service to non-subscribers.

    The Union Library Catalogue is prepared to furnish specific
    library locations represented by its symbol PPULC in the
    published National Union Catalog. Direct services are not
    available to out-of-state libraries or organizations on a
    regular basis.

TENNESSEE

Union Catalog of Books in Nashville Libraries

Joint University Libraries

Nashville, Tenn. 37203

Tel 615-254-1429, ex 7387   TWX 810-371-1224   Director Frank Grisham
II libraries; 724,046 cards; 34,368 added last year.

Includes: University, special, public and state libraries.

Description: Main entry catalog for separates and serials, author
    analytics, cross references.

Non-member service: Location service available without fee to
    individuals and libraries.

VERMONT

Free Public Library Service

Montpelier, Vermont 05602

Tel 802-223-2311, ex 548 TWX 710-225-1772 Exec.Sec. Mrs.
    Lillian Irons

233 libraries; 858,943 cards; 65,588 cards added last year.

Includes: Larger public, college, and university libraries in the state.

Non-member service: Location information without fee.

WASHINGTON

Pacific Northwest Bibliographic Center

University of Washington Library

Seattle, Washington 98105

Tel 206-543-1878 Director Mollie Hollreigh

40 libraries; 3,900,000 cards; 265,000 cards added last year.

Includes: Almost all the major university, college and public libraries in Washington, Oregon, Montana, Idaho and British Columbia.

Description: Main entry catalog of books and other printed materials, and some manuscripts.

Non-member service: Within the region the Center restricts service to member libraries only (approximately 200 libraries are supporting members). For libraries outside the region, it waives this rule and gives any help it can within reason, such as checking the Union Catalog for locations. There is no fee.

CANADA

Union Catalogue Division

Reference Branch

National Library

Ottawa, 2, Canada

Tel 613-996-2150 TWX 610-562-1657 Chief of UCD Mrs. Lois Burrell

293 libraries; 5,000,000 cards; 893,722 cards added last year.

Includes: Major academic, public and special libraries of Canada.

Description: Main entry catalog.

Service: No fees or membership. Any individual or institution can ask for book locations or bibliographic information.

ACADEMIC LIBRARIES SUPPLEMENT TO

DIRECTORY OF INSTITUTIONAL PHOTOCOPYING SERVICES

(INCLUDING SELECTED INTERLIBRARY LOAN POLICIES)

The new edition of Cosby Brinkley's Directory of Institutional
Photocopying Services (Including Selected Interlibrary Loan Policies)[1]
is being restricted to institutions with significant photocopying
facilities and/or research collections. Some academic institutions
not meeting the qualification of having significant photocopying
facilities may, nevertheless, be making significant contributions as
interlibrary lenders; therefore selected academic institutions, not
included in the Brinkley Directory, that replied to his questionnaire
have been included here.

    The interlibrary loan questions were:

    1. NUC symbol 2. Complete name and address to which ILL requests
should be sent. 3. Serials not lent if reference less than _____
pages. 4. Dissertations accepted between _____ (date) and
_____ (date) are available for loan. 5. Dissertations accepted by
our university since _____ (date) have been microfilmed by:
a. _____ University Microfilms b. _____ Ourselves.
6. TWX number, if requests are so accepted. 7. Microfilm can be
supplied at _____ per exposure. 8. Direct reading copies (Xerox or
other) can be supplied at _____ per exposure.

_____

    [1]Chicago, 1969.

CU -A   Interlibrary Loan
        UNIVERSITY OF CALIFORNIA AT DAVIS
        Davis, Calif 95616
                3. 10 pages),. through Dec. 1959. 5. To May 196), by
                Univ. Calif. Photographic Service, University of California
                at Berkeley; since June 196),, by UM. 8. 8 1/2 x 11: 15
                cents; 11x 1), 20 cents, plus service charge of *1.35.

CoCC   Interlibrary Loan Service
        Tutt Library
        COLORADO COLLEGE
        Colorado Springs, Colorado 80903
                3. Serials not lent. 8. 10 cents per page.

CoCA   U. S. AIR FORCE ACADEMY LIBRARY
        Attn: Interlibrary Loan
        U. S. Air Force Academy, Colorado 808),0
                3. 10 pages.),. Since 1955.

CtU   Reference Department
        Wilbur Cross Library
        UNIVERSITY OF CONNECTICUT
        Storrs, Connecticut 06268
                3. 20 pages.),. 1953 to 1968. 5. 1953 UM.
                6. 710-),),0-0603. 8. 15 cents per exposure

CtW   Interlibrary Loan Office
        Olin Library
        WESLEYAN UNIVERSITY
        Middletown, Conn. 06),57
                3. Serials not lent.),. Not available. 8. 10 cents per
                page, minimum order *1.50.

DGW   GEORGE WASHINGTON UNIVERSITY
        Interlibrary Loans
        2023 G Street, N.W.
        Washington, D. C. 20006
                3. Serials not lent.),. Through 1965. 5. Since 1966,
                UM. 6. 710-822-9278. 8. 10 cents per exposure.

FMU   Interlibrary Loans
        UNIVERSITY OF MIAMI LIBRARY
        Coral Gables, Florida 3312),
                3. 10 pages.),. All 5. 1959- UM. 8. 10 cents per page,
                minimum order *1.00.

IdU   Interlibrary Loans
        UNIVERSITY OF IDAHO LIBRARY
        Moscow, Idaho 838),3
                3,), pages.),. Not loaned. 5. UM. 8. 10 cents per page.

InNd   Memorial Library
        UNIVERSITY OF NOTRE DAME
        Notre Dame, Indiana),6556
                ),. Prior to 1952. 5. Since 1952, UM. 8. 8 cents for
                first 10 copies; 5 cents for 11 or more copies, plus 10
                cents service charge.

KEmT   Interlibrary Loans
        White Library
        KANSAS STATE TEACHERS COLLEGE
        Emporia, Kansas 66801
            6. 910-710-1665. 8. 10 cents per exposure

KMK   Interlibrary Loans
        KANSAS STATE UNIVERSITY LIBRARY
        Manhattan, Kansas 66502
            3. 20 pages. 4. 1941-1955. 5. Since 1955, UM.
            6. 910-719-6528. 8. 10 cents per page, minimum of
        50 cents per order.

MA   Interlibrary Loans
        AMHERST COLLEGE LIBRARY
        Amherst, Mass. 01002
            3. 40 pages. 8. 10 cents per exposure, 1.00 minimum
        per order.

MSM   Interlibrary Loan
        MOUNT HOLYOKE COLLEGE LIBRARY
        South Hadley, Massachusetts 01075
            3. 10 pages. 4. All 8. 10 cents per page, *1.00 minimum
        per order.

MNS   Reference Department
        SMITH COLLEGE LIBRARY
        Northampton, Massachusetts 01060
            3. Current issue not lent. 4. All. 8. Up to 10 pages
        free, after that 10 cents per exposure.

MMeT   TUFTS UNIVERSITY LIBRARY
        Medford, Mass. 02155
            4. Lent if have circulating copy. 5. June 1968, UM.
            6. 10 cents per exposure, minimum order 1.00.

MU   Interlibrary Loan Service
        University Library
        UNIVERSITY OF MASSACHUSETTS
        Amherst, Massachusetts 01002
            3. 50 pages. 4. Through 1961. 5. Since 1961, UM.
            6. 710-369-6430. 8. 5 cents per page.

NhD   Interlibrary Loan Department
        Baker Library
        DARTMOUTH COLLEGE
        Hanover, N. H. 03755
            3. 10 pages. 4. 1964 to date. 5. 1964 UM.
            6. 710-366-1829 8. First 10 pages free, then 8 cents
        per exposure.

NNCoCi Interlibrary Loan
        CITY COLLEGE LIBRARY
        135th Street and Convent Avenue
        New York, New York 10031
            3. Serials not lent unless little used and over 30 years
        old. 4. Questions concerning dissertations should be
        directed to Graduate Center, 33 West 42nd Street, New York,
        N.Y. 10036, c/o Interlibrary Loan. 6. 212-640-5033.
        8. 10 cents per exposure.

NHC Interlibrary Loan
COLGATE UNIVERSITY LIBRARY
Hamilton, New York 13346
    3. 20 pages. 8. 10 cents after first 20 pages.

NNC-T TEACHERS COLLEGE LIBRARY
Columbia University
New York, New York 10027
    3. Serials not lent. 4. Ph.D. through 1949; Ed.D. through 1962. 5. Ph.D. 1950 and later, Ed.D. 1963 and later, UM.
    6. 710-581-4433. 8. 10 cents per exposure plus $1.00 handling.

NNF Interlibrary Services
FORDHAM UNIVERSITY LIBRARY
Bronx, New York 10458
    3. Serials not lent. 4. 1933-1961. 5. Since 1961, UM.
    8. 10 cents per exposure, minimum order $1.00.

NTR Interlibrary Loan, Reference Section
RENSSELAER POLYTECHNIC INSTITUTE LIBRARY
Troy, N. Y. 12181
    4. Through 1953. 5. Since 1954, UM. 8. 10 cents per exposure, plus minimum of 25 cents postage and handling.

NcRS D. H. Hill Library
NORTH CAROLINA STATE UNIVERSITY
P. O. Box 5007
Raleigh, North Carolina 27607
    3. Serials not lent. 4. Approximately 1900-1956.
    5. Since 1956, UM. 8. 8 1/2 x 11: 10 cents, 9x14: 15 cents; minimum charge per order $1.00. Service charge 50 cents per order.

OClCS Interlibrary Loan Department
Sears Library
CASE Western Reserve University
10900 Euclid Avenue
Cleveland, Ohio 44106
    3. Serials not lent. 4. Prior to 1954. 5. Since 1954, UM.
    8. 20 cents per page, 25 cents mailing charge, minimum $1.00 per order.

OClW Interlibrary Loan Librarian
Freiberger Library
Case WESTERN RESERVE UNIVERSITY
Cleveland, Ohio 44106
    3. Serials not lent. 4. Prior to Sept., 1964. 5. Since Sept. 1964, UM. 6. 810-421-8818 Identification name is CLEV RG UN CAT (Cleveland Regional Union Catalog.)
    8. 10 cents per page, $1.00 service charge, $1.00 minimum per order.

OO OBERLIN COLLEGE LIBRARY
Oberlin, Ohio 44074
Attn. Head, Readers Service
    3. 10-15 pages. 8. 10 cents per exposure, 25 cents charge for postage, unless unusually bulky quantity, in which case more. If very lengthy, may add service charge per hour required to copy.

OkS   Interlibrary Loan Service
OKLAHOMA STATE UNIVERSITY LIBRARY
Stillwater, Oklahoma 74074
        3. Serials not lent. 4. Through 1961. 5. Since 1961, UM.
        6. 910-831-3178 through OK DEPT OF LIBS (Oklahoma Dept.
        of Libraries). 8. 10 cents per page, plus service charge
        of about 10%.

PBm   Interlibrary Loans
BRYN MAWR COLLEGE LIBRARY
Bryn Mawr, Pennsylvania 19010
        3. Serials not lent. 4. Dissertations from 1885 to date
        lent if library has printed or microfilm copy. 5. Some,
        but not all, since 1952 microfilmed by UM. 8. 15 cents
        per exposure, plus charge for first class postage.

ScU   Reference Department
McKissick Memorial Library
UNIVERSITY OF SOUTH CAROLINA
Columbia, S. C. 29208
        3. Serials not lent. 4. Before 1953. 5. Since 1953, UM.
        8. 10 cents per exposure, minimum charge $1.00

TxWB   BAYLOR UNIVERSITY LIBRARY
Box 6307
Waco, Texas 76706
        3. 10 pages, Xerox copy furnished automatically.
        4. Beginning to 1963, condition permitting. 5. Since
        September, 1964, UM. 8. 10 cents exposure

TxCM   Interlibrary Loans- Lending
TEXAS A & M UNIVERSITY
College Station, Texas 77840
        3. 50 pages. 4. Up to 1963. 5. Since 1963, UM.
        6. 910-880-4425. 8. 10 cents per page.

TxHU   Interlibrary Loans
Library
UNIVERSITY OF HOUSTON
Houston, Texas 77004
        3. 20 pages. 4. Any date if library has circulating copy.
        5. Since 1954, UM. 6. 910-881-3754. 8. 10 cents per
        exposure, plus $1.00 search fee and $3.00 minimum for
        companies only.

TxU   Tarlton Law Library
UNIVERSITY OF TEXAS
2500 Red River
Austin, Texas 78705
        3. Some serials not lent. 8. 10 cents per page.

TxU-M   University of Texas
MEDICAL BRANCH LIBRARY
Galveston, Texas 77550
        3. 50 pages. 4. Not lent, special Xerox rates.
        6. 910-885-5225. 8. First 10 exposures free, then
        10 cents per page, minimum charge $1.10.

ULA   Interlibrary Loan
       UTAH STATE UNIVERSITY
       Logan, Utah 84321
              3. 25 pages. 4. 1950-1958 5. 1958 UM.
              6. 910-971-5872. 8. 10 cents per exposure, 1-24; 8 cents
              per exposure 25-49; 6 cents per exposure after 50.

VtU   Interlibrary Loan Service
       UNIVERSITY OF VERMONT
       Burlington, Vermont 05401
              3. 10 pages. 4. All. 6. 710-224-6774. 8. Up to 10
              exposures free, 10 cents per exposure after that.

VtU-M Interlibrary Loan
       DANA MEDICAL LIBRARY
       University of Vermont
       Burlington, Vermont 05401
              3. 20 pages. 6. 710-224-6774.

WaPS   WASHINGTON STATE UNIVERSITY LIBRARY
       Pullman, Washington 99163
              3. 13 pages. 4. Up to 1956. 5. Since 1956 UM.
              8. 10 cents per page.

Bibliography

This is a highly selective bibliography including articles on interlibrary loan judged to be still useful for more detailed information than can be covered in this manual, on related instructional manuals and directories, and for background information. Readers interested in the historical development of interlibrary loan are referred to the bibliography by Pings cited below.

"[ALA] Council Takes Stand on Copyright Legislation," *ALA Bulletin* 62:275–77 (March 1968).

ALA RSD Interlibrary Loan Committee. "International Interlibrary Loan Procedure for United States Libraries." 2d rev. June 1963. Mimeographed. Available from ALA Headquarters Library.

Ash, Lee, and Bruette, Vernon R. *Interlibrary Request and Loan Transactions among Medical Libraries of the Greater New York Area.* New York: Survey of Medical Library Resources of Greater New York, 1966.

ASTM Coden for Periodical Titles. Philadelphia: American Society for Testing and Materials, 1967 (DS 23A).

Atwood, Ruth. "An Anemometer for I.L.L. Winds," *College and Research Libraries* 29:285–91 (July 1968).

Bird, Warren. *Teletypewriter Exchange System for Interlibrary Communication.* [Durham, N.C.: Duke University Medical Center Library] July 1969.

———— "TWX and Interlibrary Loans," *Medical Library Association Bulletin* 57:125–29 (April 1969).

———— and Skene Melvin, David, compilers. *Library Telecommunications Directory: Canada–United States.* 3d ed. rev. Durham, N.C.: Duke University Medical Center Library; London, Ontario: Canadian Library Association. Library Mechanization Committee, 1969.

Black, Dorothy M. *Guide to Lists of Master's Theses.* Chicago: American Library Association, 1965.

Boylan, Nancy G. "Identifying Technical Reports through U.S. Government Research Reports and Its Published Indexes," *College and Research Libraries* 28:175–83 (May 1967).

Brinkley, Cosby, comp. *Directory of Institutional Photocopying Services (Including Selected Interlibrary Loan Policies).* Chicago, 1969. (Available from Photoduplication Service, Swift Hall, University of Chicago, Chicago, Ill. 60637.)

Brummel, Leendert, and Egger, E. *Guide to Union Catalogues and International Loan Centers.* Published under the auspices of the International Federation of Library Associations (IFLA). The Hague: Nijhoff, 1961.

111

Budington, W. S. "Administrative Aspects of Interlibrary Loans," *Special Libraries* 55:211–15 (April 1964).

Cassidy, Thomas R. "The National Library of Medicine and Interlibrary Loan," *Medical Library Association Bulletin* 55:390–93 (Oct. 1967).

Clapp, Verner. *Copyright: A Librarian's View.* Washington: Association of Research Libraries, 1968.

———— "Copyright Dilemma: A Librarian's View," *Library Quarterly* 38:352–87 (Oct. 1968).

Estes, David Edgar. "Interlibrary Loan Practices in the Southeastern Area," *Southeastern Librarian* 13:32–41 (Spring 1963).

" 'Fair Use' under Copyright Faces Court Test," *ALA Bulletin* 62:616 (June 1968).

Federal Libraries Interlibrary Loan Code. Washington, D.C.: Federal Library Committee, Library of Congress, 1968.

Freehafer, Edward G. "Summary Statement of Policy of the Joint Libraries Committee on Fair Use in Photocopying," *Special Libraries* 55:104–106 Feb. 1964).

Gatliff, Jane W., and Foreman, S. "Interlibrary Loan Policies on Dissertations and Serial Publications," *College and Research Libraries* 25:209–11 (May 1964).

Hawken, William R. *Copying Methods Manual.* (LTP Publications no.11). Chicago: Library Technology Program, American Library Association, 1966.

Heron, D. W. "Photocopy and Interlibrary Loan," *RQ* 4:3–4 (Jan. 1965).

Hirsch, F. E. "Interlibrary Loans from the College Viewpoint," *College and Research Libraries* 10:434–39 (Oct. 1949).

Hutchins, Margaret. *Introduction to Reference Work.* Chicago: American Library Association, 1944. (See especially pages 41–51, 190–91.)

"Interlibrary Loan Code for the Philadelphia Area," in Special Libraries Council of Philadelphia and Vicinity, *Directory of Libraries and Information Sources in the Philadelphia Area,* p.126–31. Philadelphia: The Council, 1964.

"Interlibrary Loan Developments," *RQ* 7:111–25 (Spring, 1968).

Joint Libraries Committee on Copyright. "Library Position on Copyright Law Revision," *Library Journal* 90:3403–3405 (Sept. 1, 1965).

Keenan, Elizabeth L. "Interlibrary Loan, 1952–62: Ten Years of Progress?" *Medical Library Association Bulletin* 52:307–15 (Jan. 1964).

Kinney, Mary R. *The Abbreviated Citation—A Bibliographical Problem.* (ACRL Monograph no.28). Chicago: American Library Association, 1967.

Kuncaitis, Yadwiga. *Union Catalogs and Bibliographic Centers: A State-of-the-Art Review.* Columbus, Ohio: The State Library of Ohio, 1968.

"Lending to Reprinters: Policy Statement of the Reprinting Committee," *Library Resources and Technical Services* 12:455–56 (Fall 1968).

"Librarian, What of the Undergrad? Interlibrary Loan Debate," *RQ* 6:158–63 (Summer 1967).

Morehouse, Harold G. "The Future of Telefacsimile in Libraries: Problems and Prospects," *Library Resources and Technical Services* 13:42–46 (Winter 1969).

Nelson Associates, Inc. *The New York State Library's Pilot Program in the Facsimile Transmission of Library Materials: A Summary Report.* New York: Nelson Associates, 1968.

———— *Prospects for Library Cooperation in New York City; Planning for More Effective Utilization of Reference and Research Resources.* New York: Nelson Associates, 1963.

Oehlerts, Donald E. *Study to Determine the Feasibility of Establishing a Coopera-tive Technical Processing Program and Direct Transmission of Interlibrary Loans.* Denver: Association of State Institutions of Higher Education in Colo-rado, 1962.

Pacific Northwest Bibliographic Center. *Manual of Information for Participating Libraries.* Rev. ed. Seattle: The Center, 1966.

Pings, Vern M. *Interlibrary Loans, a Review of the Literature, 1876–1965.* Detroit: Wayne State University, School of Medicine Library, 1966.

Plotkin, J. "Dissertations and Interlibrary Loan," *RQ* 4:5–9 (Jan. 1965).

Ratcliffe, T. E., Jr. "Observations on the Current Practice of Interlibrary Lending," *Special Libraries* 55:207–11 (April 1964).

Reynolds, M. M. "Photocopy Policy Studied," *RQ* 5:23–24 (Summer 1966).

Roberts, Matt. "Copyright and Photocopying: An Experiment in Cooperation," *College and Research Libraries,* 30:222–29 (May 1969).

Roe, J. H., and Cassidy, T. R. "Interlibrary Loan Service of the National Library of Medicine," *College and Research Libraries* 26:45–48 (Jan. 1965).

Schwegmann, George A., Jr. "Some Speculations on the Future of the Interlibrary Loan," *Special Libraries* 55:216–20 (April 1964).

Skipper, James E. "ARL Survey of the Availability of Research Library Materials." Mimeographed. Washington: Association of Research Libraries, 1965.

Staples, Emeline R. "Interlibrary Lending of Periodicals," *Southeastern Librarian* 16:32–35 (Spring 1966).

Stephanie, Sister M. "History of the Interlibrary Loan Code," *Wisconsin Library Bulletin* 57:272–75 (Sept. 1961).

Thomson, Sarah Katharine. "General Interlibrary Loan Services in Major Academic Libraries in the United States." D.L.S. dissertation, Columbia University, 1967. Ann Arbor, Michigan: University Microfilms, 1968 (order no. 68-8558).

"TWX at NLM," *Medical Library Association Bulletin* 54:446–47 (Oct. 1966).

U.S. Department of Health, Education and Welfare. Public Health Service. *Survey of the Interlibrary Loan Operation of the National Library of Medicine,* by William H. Kurth. Washington, D.C.: Govt. Print. Off., 1962.

U.S. Library of Congress. General Reference and Bibliography Division. *Union Lists of serials; a bibliography.* Compiled by Ruth S. Freitag. Washington: 1964.

——— Union Catalog Division. *Symbols of American Libraries.* 10th ed. Wash-ington, D.C.: Library of Congress, 1969.

United States of America Standards Institute. *USA Standard for Periodical Title Abbreviations.* New York: USASI, 1964 (Z39.5-1963).

Waldeck, F. "Source of Irreverence: ULS," *Library Resources and Technical Ser-vices* 9:243–44 (Spring 1965).

Winchell, Constance M. *Locating Books for Interlibrary Loan.* New York: H. W. Wilson Co., 1930.

Index

Abbreviations: in citations, 23, 35; of sources of verification, 21, 93–97

Academic libraries directory supplement, 105–10

Acknowledgment, *see* Reports

Acquisitions: cooperative, 9–12; photocopy, 51

Addresses: borrowing library's address, teletype requests, 56; college and university libraries directory supplement, 105–10; lending library's address on request forms, 27–28; union catalogs and bibliographic centers directory, 98–104

Airmail, 27, 48

ALA Interlibrary Loan Request form, *see* Interlibrary Loan Request form

ALA policy on photocopy, 49–50

Alphabets, non-Roman, 22, 37–38

Anonymous works, citation of, 29

Answerback codes, teletype, 54

Author entry, see Bibliographic citation

Bibliographic centers, *see* Union catalogs and bibliographical centers

Bibliographic citation, 5, 22–23; use of Library of Congress entry, 21, 23. *See examples by form*: Books, 29; Dissertations, 30, 31; Government documents, 30, 31; Master's essays, 30, 31; Newspapers on microfilm, 37; Non-Roman alphabet requests, 37–38; Pamphlets, 29; Periodical articles, 35–36; Serials, 35–36; Technical reports, 31–35

Bibliographic collections: responsibility of each library to develop, 5, 22. *See also* Reference referral systems and resource libraries

Bibliographical centers, *see* Union catalogs and bibliographical centers

Book collections, responsibility of each library to develop, 2, 5, 9–10

Books: citation, verification, and request form, 29; in current and recurring demand, 12; in print, 3–4

Borrowing libraries, eligibility, ix

Borrowing library's address, teletype requests, 56

Borrowing policy, 19–20, 85–86

Brinkley, *Directory of Institutional Photocopying Services (Including Selected Interlibrary Loan Policies)*, 25, 40, 105–10

Budget, *see* Costs

Canadian loans, 66

"Cannot verify," 5

Carbons, to remain in ILL forms, 39

Card catalog searching, 45

Cartons, *see* Shipping

Channeling requests, *see* Reference referral systems and resource libraries

Chargeback arrangements, 13–15, 55–56

Citations, *see* Bibliographic citations

Class use, borrowing for, 10, 11, 13

Code, *see* IFLA International Loan Code; Model Interlibrary Loan Code for Regional, State, Local, or Other Special Groups of Libraries; National Interlibrary Loan Code

Collections, *see* Bibliographic collections; Book collections

College and university libraries directory supplement, 105–10

Computer networks, 1

Cooperative activities, 48. *See also* Acquisitions; Delivery services; Deposit accounts for photocopy; Model Interlibrary Loan Code; Reciprocal arrangements; Reciprocal direct lending to individuals; Reference referral systems and resource libraries; Union catalogs and bibliographical centers; Union lists of serials

Cooperative library systems, *see* Reference referral systems and resource libraries

Copies, *see* Photocopying

Copyright law: and library photocopy policy, 49–50; and national code, 5

Corporate entry, 29

Costs, 13–14; for borrowing library, 4; for lending library, 4; photocopy, 37–39, 50–51; shipping, 4, 39. *See also* Reciprocal arrangements

Courier routes, 15, 48

Credit transfer arrangements, 13–15, 55–56

Damage to materials, 4

Date due, 6, 47

Date of publication in citation, 29

Definition of interlibrary loan: model code, 9; national code, 1

Delay in receipt reports, 7

Delivery services, ix, 15, 48

Deposit accounts for photocopy, 50–51

Directory supplement of college and university libraries, 105–10

Directory of Institutional Photocopying Services (Including Selected Interlibrary Loan Policies), x, 25, 39, 105–10

Directory of Union Catalogs and Bibliographic Centers, 98–104

Dissertations: acquisition of, on microfilm, 63–65; borrowing and lending policy for, 3–4, 25; citation, verification, and request